THE HOLY SPIRIT LORD AND LIFE-GIVER

A Biblical Introduction to the Doctrine of the Holy Spirit

by
JOHN WILLIAMS

Prepared for

- Personal Bible Study
- Group Studies
- Sermon Series

LOIZEAUX BROTHERS
Neptune, New Jersey

FIRST EDITION, SEPTEMBER 1980

ISBN 0-87213-952-2
PRINTED IN THE UNITED STATES OF AMERICA

COURSE OUTLINE

Also Included:

PREFACE

The purpose of this *Study Guide* is to help you discover fresh insights in what the Bible teaches about your Divine Friend, the Holy Spirit. This guide is itself based on the book, *The Holy Spirit: Lord and Life-Giver*, which is a fairly comprehensive study of the doctrine of the Holy Spirit. It is the author's hope and prayer that those who pursue this course of study will end up not simply as better informed people but as Christians devoted to our Lord Jesus, determined to make their lives fully available to His Holy Spirit.

Methods of Study

This *Study Guide* can be used in various ways. For example:
- As an aid to personal study.
- As a text for group study.
- As an accompanying text for a series of sermons.

It is for you to decide just how it can serve you best. Obviously, while it can be used independently of the text on which it is based, *The Holy Spirit: Lord and Life-Giver*, it will be much more effective if used in close conjunction with it. The following guidelines are merely suggestions for those who feel they need them. There are many people who have developed their own study methods and for them this guide will simply be an additional tool.

Aid to Personal Study

1. *Time*

First decide how much time you wish to allocate to this course of study (i.e., daily, weekly, etc.). Recognize that it will be fairly demanding and that your study will require discipline and prayer.

2. *Tools*

You need a copy of the book, *The Holy Spirit: Lord and Life-Giver*, and a Bible you do not mind marking. It would be good to have a King James Version and a modern version (perhaps the NIV), a loose-leaf notebook and pen, as well as some scrap paper, an English dictionary, and pocket concordance (many Bibles have these built in).

3. *Tips*

- Try not to "bite off more than you can chew."
- Undue hurry will rob you of blessing.
- Recognize that this is not simply an academic exercise but a spiritual one.

5

•Don't be too alarmed if you meet ideas and statements with which you do not, at present, agree. The author has attempted to avoid being dogmatic but at the same time has taken a pretty firm line. He has attempted to be scriptural. Check him out!

•Begin to "respond" to the Lord's promptings as you engage in this study. Cultivate the attitude, "Lord, what wilt Thou have me to do?" (Acts 9:6) Share what you learn and get involved in the life of your church. Try to get a friend into this study. You may even decide to start a group study.

Group Study
1. *Preparatory*
•If you decide to use this guide in a group situation, make sure you are thoroughly familiar with the textbook, *The Holy Spirit: Lord and Life-Giver*.

•Be sure you plan your course and organize your sessions.

•Encourage your group members to think carefully about their commitment to this course and advise them that basically they will get out of it only what they put into it. Actually they'll get much more, especially as you, their leader, make yourself available to the Lord and to them.

•Do not doubt your ability to handle this course. Sometimes it may be tough and you may feel unworthy, but if the Lord has clearly led you into this situation, He'll see you through!

•At the outset spell out your overall plan and desires. If you know that someone in the group is a confirmed controversialist or monopolizer, be firm with him. Explain that your group meets to learn and grow but not for profitless argument (2 Timothy 2:14). By the way, explain that the course can be studied privately.

•When there is genuine dissent or variety of interpretation, encourage people to be tolerant, honest, and Biblical—agree to differ! If your group is associated with a Bible-believing church (and this we highly recommend!), should controversial matters arise, then consult your leaders and be guided by their wise counsels. Do not start factions or splinter groups. That would be a denial of what this course is all about.

2. *Tools*
Encourage each group member to have his or her copy of *The Holy Spirit: Lord and Life-Giver*, a study guide, a Bible (you may want to decide on a particular version for your group study sessions), notebooks, pencils, concordance, Bible dictionary, a dependable one-volume Bible commentary. (A coffee pot can also be a great help!)

3. *Time*
Set a definite time and period weekly for your study. Keep to your schedule and warn the group at the outset about the duration of the course and similar details. Punctuality at the beginning and end is a primary courtesy.

4. *Venue*

Some groups meet at the same place weekly, others circulate around the homes represented by the group. Decide which is best suited to your people. Involvement is a good thing and some folk may be better at doing than talking. If you are the study leader then delegate as much of the organizing and practical items as possible. This is very important.

5. *Study Time*

• You will probably need one hour for each study session.

• Begin with a brief share-and-prayer time—not more than 8 minutes. This is good preparation. Make sure people do not start arriving 8 minutes late.

• Read the Scripture portion aloud (preferably by a group member.)

• Review (5 minutes) then give a brief overview of today's lesson.

• Now go through the lesson fairly deliberately 20-25 minutes (encourage people to save questions till later).

• You may want to make overhead transparencies from the visuals in the guide, to use as you go through lessons. A one-page visual aid for each study is included in the center of this guide. Open staples carefully before removing visuals.

• Now use 15-20 minutes for reaction and feedback.

  -Watch for talkers and encourage considerateness.

  -Keep the discussion firmly on track.

  -Encourage participation. Do not use expressions like, "What a dumb question!" or "You couldn't be more wrong!" etc.

  -Rather be an encourager, e.g., "Thanks for that question Bill, let's think about that." If necessary suggest dealing with a topic privately over a cup of coffee.

  -You may want to encourage other members of the group to be responsible for the "Introduction of this Week's Subject." However, you should always be prepared and unobtrusively in charge.

  -Have good stimulating leading questions available.

  -Point out to your group that their best preparation for your lesson will be to read the textbook *The Holy Spirit: Lord and Life-Giver* and related Scriptures *before* they attend class.

  -You will see that there is a memory verse with each lesson.

Sermon Series

Obviously those who decide to use this approach are experienced people and quite capable of devising their own methodology. It is recommended that if this course of study is adopted, the total service programs (order of service) be arranged around the sermon topic for the day. The congregation should be encouraged to "prepare for next week" by reading the appropriate chapters in *The Holy Spirit: Lord and Life-Giver*. The preacher may decide to recruit assistants to lead home group studies in conjunction with his series of sermons. The group would either prestudy "next Sunday's lesson" or review "last Sunday's lesson." There is value in both approaches.

Final Word

The important thing is to use this guide as a tool. Do not be pressured by its format. If you want to take two sessions on a particular topic by all means do so. The main point is not to get through the lesson but to let the Lord get through to you.

Remember, *"God is . . . Spirit*: and they that worship Him must worship Him in spirit and in truth" (John 4:24).

Study 1

GETTING OUR BEARINGS / Scripture: Psalm 139
Memory: Ephesians 3:16
Textbook: Preface

In your introductory lesson on *The Holy Spirit: Lord and Life-Giver* you should (encourage your group to) recognize several things.

1. *The subject of the Holy Spirit* should be studied prayerfully, carefully, honestly, Biblically, humbly, practically, and expectantly.

2. *The doctrine of the Holy Spirit* is one of the great doctrines of our Christian faith. We usually call it pneumatology. This comes from the Greek root word *pneuma*, which means "breath," "wind," "spirit," etc. We find this root in English words like "pneumatic tire," which means "a tire filled with air."

Note that the great basic doctrines of the Christian faith include:
- God—Theology
- Christ—Christology
- Work of Christ—Atonement
- Man and Sin—Anthropology
- Salvation—Soteriology
- Scripture—Revelation and Inspiration
- Church—Ecclesiology
- Future—Eschatology
- Holy Spirit—Pneumatology

3. *The doctrine of the Holy Spirit* is not something the Church has only recently discovered. We must avoid the thought that we "modern" Christians are the only ones who have "arrived" in this matter. In fact, we need not only to think Biblically but also historically when discussing the doctrine of the Holy Spirit. In this, as in most doctrinal matters, we would be spared untold harm if we made ourselves more aware of church history, especially of the great theological debates of the early centuries (up to A.D. 500). It is a good thing to avoid extravagant twentieth-century "discoveries" in the area of pneumatology. Refer to textbook Appendix for a very brief introduction to the history of the doctrine of the Holy Spirit.

4. *There is always a danger of substituting experience* (either our own or other people's) for the peerless revelation of Scripture. No one's experience (not even the saintliest person you know) is an infallible criterion of truth.

5. *There is the ever-present temptation* in doctrinal studies to adopt the "Little Jack Horner" method of Bible interpretation. Remember,
> He put in his thumb
> And pulled out a plum
> And said: "What a good boy am I!"

We must not drag texts (verses or phrases of Scripture) out of their context. Further, we must not use unrelated verses of Scripture in our attempt to score in a debate with an opponent. (The process may backfire!) Always seek the totality of scriptural testimony.

6. *We must research the truth* concerning the Holy Spirit with a view to obeying His promptings and glorifying Christ. Jesus said, "If you know these things, happy are you if you do them" (John 13:17). (Note the Living Bible paraphrase of this verse)

7. *A properly focused study* of the doctrine of the Holy Spirit will do several things:
- •Lead you to Christ
- •Challenge you to study the Scriptures
- •Unite you with fellow Christians
- •Make you a down-to-earth person
- •Guard you from strange excesses
- •Make you settled and content in the Lord
- •Produce fruit in your life (Galatians 5:22)

(If your study is not doing this or even producing opposite effects you have good grounds to be suspicious about the direction in which you are going.)

CREDAL STATEMENTS

ARTICLE V
of the 39 Articles of Religion
The Book of Common Prayer

> The Holy Ghost, proceeding from the Father and the Son, is of one substance, majesty, glory, with the Father and the Son, very and eternal God.

From the Creed of Athanasius, known as "Quicunque vult" (Latin for the opening words, "Whosoever will")

> The Father is made of none neither created nor begotten. The Son is of the Father alone: not made, nor created, but begotten.
>
> The Holy Ghost is of the Father and of the Son, neither made, nor created, nor begotten, but proceeding.

From the Nicene Creed

> The Holy Ghost, the Lord and Giver of Life, who proceeded from the Father, who, with the Father and the Son together, is worshipped and glorified, who spoke by the prophets.

BREATH
OF GOD

/ Scripture: Ezekiel 37
Memory: 1 Corinthians 3:17
Textbook: pages 17-23

The purpose of instruction based on the next four studies should be to encourage students to familiarize themselves with the Biblical data concerning the Holy Spirit. Too many Christians think of the Holy Spirit as an impersonal influence or as if He were of lesser rank in the Godhead than the Father and the Son.

Group leaders: Explain that the title of the book is a quotation from the famous Nicene Creed. (See textbook pages 299-300.)

Read study headings aloud and explain very briefly what they are about.

Introduction to Studies 2, 3, 4, and 5
Study 2. *Breath of God*
This study deals with many of the names given to the Holy Spirit in the Old and New Testaments. In the Bible names are significant and often reflect the character and ministry of the person named.

Study 3. *Personality Plus*
The purpose of this study is to demonstrate that the Holy Spirit is a real person. Obviously this is important both for our understanding of Christian doctrine and as the basis of our knowing and experiencing the Holy Spirit.

Study 4. *Infinity*
In this study the author presents the truth of the essential deity of the Holy Spirit. He also gives a brief introduction to the relationships within the Godhead.

Study 5. *Pictures and Parables*
This study deals with the many Biblical pictures or emblems (as we usually call them) of the Holy Spirit. The pictures reveal truth about the Spirit's Person and work (i.e., who He is and what He does).

We recommend that people think carefully about the credal statements and perhaps even memorize one of them. It would be a good idea to read them over aloud (with your group).

Introductory Thought—Study 2
In our society names have little significance, except within a family context. However in Scripture names tend to be very carefully selected and signify something of a person's character or service. Of course, we are not altogether unfamiliar with a name reflecting a man's work. Even in our western society some of us have inherited names like:

Cooper—a man who made barrels
Wheeler—a man who manufactured and installed wheels
Carter—a man who carried goods
Fletcher—a man who made arrows
The list could include Painter, Potter, Baker, Butcher, all the Smiths, etc.
(Ask group to think of others)

The names of the Holy Spirit in Scripture are really some of His titles.
They do two things:
•They describe His Glorious Person. Each name is like the facet of a
diamond reflecting the light of revelation.
•They give us insight into His many activities and ministries. In Chapter 1
of the textbook, the Holy Spirit's names or titles are brought together under
various headings. These are:
•*Old Testament Names*
These fall into two categories:
  Names revealing deity.
  Names revealing attributes.
•*New Testament Names*
These stress the Holy Spirit's relation to God the Father and to Christ the
Son. They also reveal His divine attributes.
•*"Spirit"*
It is interesting to observe that in both the main languages of Scripture
the word used for "Spirit" can also describe
  "Breath" or "wind."
  The Hebrew word is *ruach*.
  The Greek word is *pneuma*.
Refer to Ezekiel 37 to see various translations of *ruach* and to John 3 for
pneuma.
Is there perhaps a reflection here of the fact that just as "breath" is an
evidence of life (for example in the phrase, "the breath of life") so the
"Spirit" is the essential source and sustainer of eternal life.
•*"Ghost"*
While this term is commonly applied to the Holy Spirit—i.e., "Holy
Ghost"—it needs explaining to our contemporaries. In 1611 when the King
James Version was made, "ghost" was a perfectly acceptable translation of
ruach or *pneuma*. The immaterial part of a person was described as his
"spirit" or "ghost." For example, a person was said to have "given up the
ghost" when he died (cf., John 19:30). However, today the word "ghost"
connotes the spooks and hobgoblins of a Halloween "trick or treat" and is
not a suitable translation.
Note also that while we can refer to the Holy Spirit as "the Spirit," we
cannot intelligibly refer to Him as "the Ghost." It is necessary always to
insert the adjective "Holy."

•*"Paraclete"*

The name Paraclete transliterates the Greek word *paraklētos* (see textbook page 22 for an explanation). A good literal translation would be "one summoned alongside." Research the translations of this word in the various modern versions. Are there other words that might also express the truth contained in this title of the Holy Spirit?

Suggested Exercises

•Take a concordance and carefully list all the Biblical names of the Holy Spirit.

•Try to analyze these names and add references.

•Discuss why there are more references to the Holy Spirit in the Old Testament than in the New Testament.

Study 3

PERSONALITY PLUS

Scripture: John 14:14-31
Memory: John 16:13
Textbook: pages 24-28

Introductory Comments

Here we are confronted with the truth of the personality of the Holy Spirit. We must not think or speak of the Spirit as an impersonal influence but as a real, vital Person.

While such an emphasis reflects Biblical teaching about the Spirit, it also reminds us that we can experience a person-to-person relationship with Him.

Essentially, this is a New Testament revelation although it is already anticipated in the Old Testament. Cf.,

Genesis 1:2—The Spirit "hovering, brooding"
Genesis 6:3—The Spirit "striving" or "contending"
Isaiah 63:10—The Spirit "grieved," etc.

Personality is not necessarily associated only with material things, e.g., a physical body. Of course, our normal experience of personality is related to visible human beings. We identify people by their faces, their voices, etc. However the real person is more than his body. So the Holy Spirit, although without a body, is nevertheless still a person.

1. Our Lord's Teaching

While Jesus referred to the Holy Spirit throughout His ministry He seems to have reserved His special revelation concerning the Spirit for the occasion of His upper room discourse. There are many reasons for this. Among them:

He wanted to prepare the disciples for His own departure.

The truth concerning the Holy Spirit was something for believers (in contrast with the world). "Spiritual things can only be discerned by spiritual men" is a scriptural principle (see 1 Corinthians 2:13 margin).

Scripture teaches that there was a direct correlation between the cross and the advent of the Spirit (John 7:39; 16:7).

Our Lord was deliberately linking the revelation of God He Himself had given with that which would now be given through the New Testament Scripture. These Scriptures would be written by the men (and their company) who were with Jesus in the upper room (John 16:13).

The Personality of the Holy Spirit—stressed by:

•*The precise language of Jesus*

Usually pronouns relating to a noun reflect the gender of the noun, e.g., The man put on his shoes (not "its" shoes). However, Jesus deliberately employs a masculine relative pronoun, "He" (*ekeinos*), when referring to the Spirit. He did not say: "That *It* may be with you," but "that *He* may be with you."

(For a grammatically accurate use of a neuter reflexive pronoun "itself" [*auto*] with *pneuma*, see Romans 8:16,26. However translators usually prefer the more theologically accurate "Himself" even there).

•Jesus uses "another" (*allon*) = "another of the same kind" rather than *heteros*, i.e., another of a different sort, e.g., the English sentence, "I sold my Chevy and bought another one" (i.e., another Chevy).

•*Paraklētos*—There is a passive mood (verb) behind this noun. Someone is being "summoned" or "called." This suggests personality. You cannot summon an influence!

2. Acts (The "Acts of the Holy Spirit")

The following personal activities of the Holy Spirit are noted in Acts:

•He is sinned against (5:3ff.)
•He speaks (13:2-4)
•He forbids (16:6-7)
•He appoints (20:28)

Check carefully to see what other personal activities are attributed to the Holy Spirit.

3. Epistles

In the Epistles the personality of the Spirit, while not specifically stated, is everywhere implied and understood.

While prayer is usually addressed to God the Father through the Son it is not inappropriate, in the light of His personality and His name as Advocate, to pray to the Holy Spirit.

Questions
1. Why is the truth of the personality of the Holy Spirit of particular encouragement to a Christian?
2. Demonstrate from Scripture why you believe in the personality of the Holy Spirit.
3. Consider the significance of "grieve" in Ephesians 4:30.

Study 4

INFINITY / Scripture: John 15:26—16:14
Memory: John 15:26
Textbook: pages 29-39

The Holy Spirit is essentially and eternally God, according to the testimony of Scripture. His deity is the same as that of the Father and of the Son. We may refer to Him as the "Third Person of the Godhead" but we must be careful not to imply by this or any other expression that He is third in rank in the Trinity.

Quote
"And in this Trinity none is afore, or after other: none is greater, or less than another" (creed of Athanasius).

1. *Divine Attributes are everywhere predicated of the Holy Spirit*
   •Omnipresence (in all places)—cf., Psalm 139:7-8
   •Omniscience (having all knowledge)—cf., Isaiah 40:13-14; 1 Corinthians 2:10-11
   •Omnipotence (having all power)—cf., Zechariah 4:6; 1 Corinthians 12:4-8,11; 2 Corinthians 3:17-18
   •Eternity—cf., Hebrews 9:14; John 14:16

2. *The Holy Spirit is identified as "God" who speaks in Scripture*—Psalm 95:7; Hebrews 3:7-9; 10:15-16
   "When the Spirit speaks, God Speaks!"

3. *Teaching of Christ and Apostles*
   Jesus implies deity of the Holy Spirit when He speaks of "blasphemy against the Holy Spirit" (Matthew 12:31-32).

4. *Divine Activities*
  •Creation
    The universe
    The animals
    Man

  •Inspiration
    Of the Messiah for service
    Of the sacred writings (Old Testament and New Testament)
    Of the prophets
    Of workmen
    Of life itself

5. *Relation to Godhead*
  •Key word, *proceeding*
  Note usual expressions used of the Persons of the Godhead.
  (Look at the Greek word—cf., Vine, etc.)
    Father—"made of none"
    Son—"begotten"
    Holy Spirit—"proceeding"
  •Eternal procession (see textbook pages 38-39)
  •N.B. Filioque clause (cf., chapter on history, pages 300-301).

Study 5

PICTURES AND PARABLES

Scripture: 2 Corinthians 1:1-11,20-22
Memory: 2 Corinthians 1:21-22
Textbook: pages 40-51

Introduction
    The key principle here is that knowledge is a process of proceeding from the known to the unknown. The unique factor here is revelation.
    The Scriptures present us with familiar symbols or pictures to enable us to understand truth about the glorious Person and work of the Holy Spirit.
    In order to understand this lesson it is a good idea to draw three columns A, B, C. Under A note the Biblical symbol, under B the references, and under C possible interpretations of the symbol. The interpretations must have Scripture support to be authentic.

1. *Pictures of the Spirit's Power*
   •*Wind*

This is a particularly appropriate symbol of the Holy Spirit because the word for "Spirit" in both Hebrew and Greek can be translated wind.

Consider carefully the three Scripture passages discussed on pages 40-42 in this connection.

This symbol stresses the following aspects of the Spirit's power:

All pervasive
Inscrutable
Irresistible
Purposeful (e.g., wind filling a sail) cf., 2 Peter 1:21
Life-giving (using the translation "breath")

Questions

Are there parallels between Ezekiel's vision and Pentecost?

What was Jesus' point in comparing the Wind and the Spirit in John 3?

How do you understand "moved" in 2 Peter 1:21? (Check several versions)

   •*Water*

Examine the various ideas about the Spirit in passages which present Him under this symbol. For example: He refreshes, He satisfies, He cleanses.

   Isaiah 44:3-4, etc.
   Explain what "poetic parallelism" means.

   Hebrew poetry tends to stress association of ideas and use of mechanical language forms, in contrast with our English use, cf., rhyme and rhythm. For example, look at the alphabetic poem, Psalm 119, where every verse in each stanza begins with the same Hebrew letter, and the stanzas progress through the Hebrew alphabet (each representing one of its 22 letters). Another favorite technique (the one employed here) is to state an idea in the first line of a couplet and then repeat it by using a different symbol or synonym in the second line. This is parallelism and is often a useful key to scriptural interpretation.

The entire book of Lamentations is written in alphabetic form. All chapters contain 22 verses, one for each letter of the Hebrew alphabet. Chapter 3 has 66 verses (i.e., 22 x 3).

   Ezekiel 36:25-27 and John 3:5-6

As we might expect, Ezekiel as a priest stresses the idea of the Spirit as a cleansing agent. The "sprinkled water" reflects the ceremony of the red heifer, in Numbers 19. The sacrifice was reduced to ashes and these ashes were kept ready to be mixed with running water and sprinkled on a person who had contracted ceremonial defilement (e.g., through contact with a dead body). Consider the spiritual significance of this in the light of Ezekiel's prophecy, John 3:5-6, and Hebrews 9:13-14.

John 7:37-38
A key passage in Jesus' teaching concerning the Holy Spirit, especially with regard to the symbol of water. Refer to textbook, pages 35-36, for details of Tabernacle ceremony.

•*Fire*
Another important symbol of the Spirit's power.
Stresses such ideas as:
  Refining
  Warming
  Destroying
  Welding together
  Illuminating
Compare John the Baptizer's prophecy with the events of Pentecost. They are clearly associated. In John's prophecy the fire is metaphorical, in Acts 2 it is "literal." At Pentecost the fire appears to be a deliberate sensory sign of the Spirit's presence. (Suggestion for Class: Draw these Bible symbols under the headings: The Spirit's Power, and The Spirit's Presence)

2. *Pictures of the Spirit's Person and Presence*
  •*Dove*—Consider Biblical references to the dove and note its associations, e.g.,
    Genesis 8:8-12
    Leviticus 12:6
    Isaiah 38:14
    Matthew 10:16
  •*Oil*—Usually associated with the idea of anointing for special service. Note those who are anointed: the cleansed leper, the prophet, the priest, the king. (Look up and write down references.) Make a special note of the method of the priest's anointing in Exodus. Read "note 3" at Exodus 27:20 in the Scofield Reference Bible.
  Consider the many ideas suggested by the use of oil as a symbol of the Spirit.
  •*Seal*—Usually symbolized possession, security, and genuineness. Note Paul's phrase in Ephesians 4:30, "sealed unto the day of redemption." He does not simply mean "until the day of redemption," but "with a view to the day of redemption." In other words, the Holy Spirit is God's mark or seal on the believer which guarantees his redemption.
  Note Jeremiah's sealed deed (Jeremiah 32:11).
  •*Earnest*—The earnest as a symbol of the Spirit suggests that, for the Christian, the Holy Spirit is a little foretaste of Heaven.
  •*Firstfruits*—Just as the firstfruits offering was a sort of promise of the full harvest and spoke of consecration to God, so the Holy Spirit is God's promise of all that's to come.

CONCEIVED OF THE HOLY GHOST

Scripture: Matthew 1:18-25
Luke 3:21-23
Memory: John 3:34
Textbook: pages 53-64

Introduction

These next two studies deal with the subject of the Holy Spirit and Revelation. Study 6 is concerned with God's revelation in the Incarnation (i.e., in Christ), and Study 7 with God's revelation through the inspired Scriptures. A grasp of this subject is essential to our understanding of the doctrine of the Holy Spirit.

A key verse

John 3:34: "For He whom God hath sent speaketh the words of God: for God giveth not the Spirit by measure unto Him."

Key Thought

Scripture teaches that the Holy Spirit was intimately and essentially involved at every point in the Saviour's life.

The Holy Spirit rested ungrieved, in all His fullness, upon the immaculate Saviour.

1. *The Nativity*—"conceived of the Holy Ghost"
•Note the well-chosen words of these key phrases concerning the virgin birth of Jesus.
    -Luke 1:35—"the power of the Highest shall overshadow thee"
    -Matthew 1:18—"Mary was ... found with child of the Holy Ghost"
    -Matthew 1:20—"that which is conceived in her is of the Holy Ghost"
•The miracle of the virgin birth is an essential part of the Biblical revelation concerning Christ. While it is impossible to explain it in terms of ordinary human existence it is also impossible to believe that such a unique person as Jesus could have been begotten as the result of natural generation.
•It is perfectly reasonable within the purview of Biblical theology, which views the Holy Spirit as the Creator of life, to see Him as the divine agent who supernaturally fashioned our Lord's body in the womb of the Virgin Mary.
•We must distinguish between incarnational myths, which deal with half-human, half-divine creatures, and the historical event of the virgin birth, which involved real human beings.

2. *Baptism*
The descent of the Holy Spirit as a dove at Jesus' baptism was:
•The Visible Sign of Jesus' anointing for service

•Confirmatory not initiatory—i.e., it demonstrated that Jesus as God's Son was full of the Holy Spirit. It was not the beginning of Jesus' Sonship nor of His experience of the Spirit. It signaled:
•The involvement of the Godhead—Father, Son, and Holy Spirit—in the Incarnation
•The gentleness, guilelessness, and purity of the Saviour.

3. *The Temptation*
This story demonstrates Christ's complete submission to the Holy Spirit in two ways:
•He is led by the Spirit.
•He depends (as Man) on the WORD inspired by the Spirit.
Consider the importance of Jesus' example for us in terms of our submission to the Holy Spirit.

4. *The ministry and miracles* (see text pages 59-60)
•The Lord Jesus was a unique vehicle of the Spirit in His impeccable humanity.
•It is important to keep in mind that Jesus was not part man and part God.
•"Two whole and perfect natures, that is to say, the Godhead and Manhood, were joined together in one Person, never to be divided, whereof is one Christ, very God and very Man" (Article II - 39 Articles).
•Beware of drawing the false conclusion that "if we only submit to the Holy Spirit as Jesus did then we can do the things He did." We are not sinless nor are we divine!

5. *The Passion*
•The Holy Spirit was involved even in our Lord's saving death.
•He ratifies the sacrifice and makes real its saving effect in the life of the believer.
•Note the words of John 7:37-38. When the rock was smitten the water flowed. When Christ died the Spirit was given (see lesson on water as emblem of the Spirit).

6. *Resurrection*
Note the Trinity is involved in our Lord's resurrection:
Romans 8:11—The Father—raises the Son
John 10:18—The Son—takes His life again
1 Peter 3:18-19—The Spirit—quickens the Son
Consider the resurrection as the greatest miracle of all and as an essential fact of our Christian faith.

7. *The Ascension*
Note the direct correlation between Jesus' ascent and the Spirit's descent.

Practical lesson (in summary)

Just as the Holy Spirit moved through all the life of our Saviour, so He wants to be filling Christ's people "in every part."

Quote

Fill Thou my life, O Lord my God,
In every part with praise
That my whole being may proclaim
Thy being and Thy ways.

Horatius Bonar 1808-1889

Study 7

MEN SPAKE FROM GOD

Scripture: Jeremiah 36
Memory: 2 Peter 1:20-21
Textbook: pages 65-74

Introduction

The doctrine of the inspiration of Scripture by the Holy Spirit is at the heart of our evangelical faith.

While "inspiration" in its precise sense describes that gracious movement of the Holy Spirit by which *revealed truth* became *written truth*, we must remember that both the Spirit and the Word are living. There is a sense then in which inspiration is historical, contemporary, and eternal.

Explain Terms
- Inspiration—"breathed out by God."
- Verbal inspiration—the actual words of the original text are God-breathed.
- Plenary inspiration—Scripture in all its parts is inspired.
- Inerrancy—Scripture not liable to error in any way.
- Infallible—Scripture is perfect and reliable.
- Revelation—divine truth communicated to men.

1. *Old Testament Inspiration*

Consider Jeremiah 36 and 2 Samuel 23:2 in support of the idea that Old Testament writers recognized their own inspiration.

New Testament writer's view: "When Scripture speaks, the Spirit speaks."

21

References: 1 Peter 1:10-11; Hebrews 9:8; Matthew 22:43; Hebrews 3:7-8.
Hebrews 9:8 supports the idea that even the pictures and symbols of the Old Testament are inspired.

Explanation

A type is usually an illustration (a thing or a person) or figure of some special truth. Many types occur in the Old Testament and are interpreted in the New Testament (these interpretations are sometimes called antitypes). See Hebrews 9:24—"figures"—Greek, *antitupa*

Type	Antitype
the Rock	Christ (1 Corinthians 10:4)
Moses' brazen serpent	Christ's sacrifice (John 3:14)
the Manna	Christ the Living Bread (John 6)

2. *Two Key Passages*
- 2 Peter 1:19-21
Note: Scripture superior to experience (even an experience like being on the Mount of Transfiguration!)
This is the most precise passage describing "inspiration" in the New Testament. Peter notes the following:
Scripture is result of revelation not meditation
Inspiration is verbal—"each prophecy" (Greek, *pasa graphē*)
Scripture was written by men
These men were "moved" (i.e., carried along like a ship) by the Holy Spirit (this guarantees inerrancy)
- 2 Timothy 3:16
Note Paul's key word *theopneustos*—"God-breathed"
Paul is not teaching "a selective inspiration" (i.e., some Scripture is inspired, some is not)
"Scripture" for Paul means "sacred, inspired writings"
The apostle is stressing the profitableness of Scripture
His phrase "every Scripture" or "each Scripture" clearly teaches plenary, verbal inspiration
We could translate him, "all [or each] Scripture being God-breathed is profitable"

3. *New Testament Inspiration*
- Jesus' Words in the upper room
"*He* will lead you *into all the truth*" is His mandate for apostles to produce New Testament canon
- The apostles' sense of inspiration (write out each verse)
1 John 4:1-6, cf., Ephesians 3:5
1 Corinthians 14:37
2 Thessalonians 2:15; 3:14
1 Peter 1:12

• Specific passages

    1 Timothy 5:18—Here a quotation from Luke's Gospel is linked with one from Deuteronomy and called "Scripture"

    1 Timothy 4:1—reflecting Matthew 24:11 or 2 Thessalonians 2:3

    Jude 17-18—reflecting 2 Peter 3:3

    Particularly 2 Peter 3:15-16, where Peter clearly states Paul wrote "Scripture"

4. *Interpretation of Scripture*

    It is suggested in several Scriptures that the Holy Spirit is the divine agent in interpretation as well as inspiration

    1 Corinthians 2:10 (margin)

    2 Corinthians 3:15-17

    1 John 5:7

    Deuteronomy 29:4

Study 8

THE CHURCH AND THE CHURCHES

Scripture: 1 Peter 2:1-10
Memory: 1 Corinthians 3:16-17
Textbook: pages 75-80

Introduction

The next five studies deal with the Holy Spirit's relationship with the Church, the mystical Body of Christ.

Studies 8 and 9 have the universal church in view while Studies 10—12 deal with the Spirit's equipping of Christians to serve in the local church.

This section of our studies also introduces us to the important subject of spiritual gifts.

We shall include a special study and work sheet at the end of Study 11, designed to help the reader/student to discover his or her spiritual gift(s).

In this study emphasis is laid on both the initial and the continuing work of the Holy Spirit in the Church.

This dual emphasis is important for two reasons:

• It recognizes that the Church is a divine institution, owing its origin to God, not man.

• It reminds us that the Church is a living, growing organism sustained not by human traditions but by the Spirit of God who indwells it.

23

1. *Incorporated by the Spirit*

•This study takes the position that, while we may see the people of God in every age as "the body of believers," the Christian Church is a distinct entity having its origin on the Day of Pentecost.

•The crucified, risen Lord ascends and, as Head of His Church, "sends forth" His Holy Spirit who unites, incorporates (forms into a body) believers into His mystical Body. Just as He had done the will of God in His physical body (incarnation), so He continues to do it through His mystical Body, the Church (see Acts 1:1).

•Note the suitability of the Day of Pentecost as the "birthday of the Church."

•Note Peter's words (Acts 11:15) where he describes the Day of Pentecost as "the beginning" (*archē*).

2. *Inspired by the Spirit*

•The Holy Spirit, who came to give birth to the Church, remains as its "life-breath."

•It is He who transforms what would otherwise be a corpse into a body.

•Conversely, where people meet as representing the monolith that is Christendom, in so-called "churches," but deny the Lordship of Christ and the power of the Spirit, there is the silence of death!

•Take note of the many references to the Holy Spirit in 1 Corinthians 12, "The Body Life chapter"—verses 3, 4, 7, 8, 9, 11, climaxing in verse 13.

•Consider the valley of dry bones miracle as a picture of a revived church (cf., Ezekiel 37).

3. *Indwelling by the Spirit*

•Another metaphor of the Church is in view here, i.e., the Church as the "temple [*naos*] of the Holy Spirit." (See Ephesians 2:21-22; 1 Corinthians 3:16-17; 1 Peter 2:5.)

•In New Testament "church" (*ekklēsia*) means *people* (living stones in a living temple), *not*:

Buildings
Organizations
Denominations
State institutions

•Characteristics of early churches:

The living presence of Christ
Submission to the Scriptures
The power of the Holy Spirit
Witness to the Risen Lord
Love for each other
(This list could be extended)

•In the local church viewed as a temple (*naos*—the Greek word for inner shrine, e.g., "holy of holies") there will be:

24

Christians fulfilling their priestly (Hosea 14:2; Hebrews 13:15) functions (worship, service, etc.)

Christians (as a "royal," "holy" priesthood) offering sacrifices to God—such as:

Romans 12:1—"their redeemed bodies—living sacrifice"
Hebrews 13:16—"doing good"
Hebrews 13:16—"sharing with those in need" (cf., James 1:27)
James 1:27
Philippians 4:18—"giving to support Christian work"

Note:

Here is a definition of the doctrine of the priesthood of all believers:

"Whereas under the Old Covenant (Old Testament) priesthood was limited to one chosen family (Aaron's), under the New Covenant (New Testament) all believers are priests together and have equally and without distinction the privilege of access to God in worship and His power made available to them for service."

Study 9

ONE PLUS ONE = ONE / Scripture: Ephesians 2:11-22
Memory: Ephesians 4:3-4
Textbook: pages 81-85

Introduction

A key passage to read at the commencement of this study would be John 17. In this, His so-called "high priestly prayer," our Lord:

prays that His disciples may be one (verse 11)
prays that we *all* may be one (verse 21)
guarantees that we shall be one (verse 22)
views His Church as ultimately perfected in one (verse 23)

Note:

What is true in fact
We must express in act.

1. *Preserving Unity*

•Paul's emphasis in Ephesians 4:3-6 matches our Lord's emphasis in His high priestly prayer.

•God the Holy Spirit has created the unity (i.e., His part); we must *preserve* it
  •Basis of Christian unity—"7 unities"
  •Consider practical ways of preserving unity among Christians today:
   In our local church
   In our city or community
  •Extremes to avoid
   Sanctimonious insularity (often defended as "guarding the purity of the truth"!)
   Syncretistic ecumenicity
   (Look up these words in a dictionary!)

2. *Unity in Diversity*

Unity does not require uniformity but communion depends on union. Paul's illustrations of the Church being like a human body exemplify this truth. Each part of a body is essential to the healthy functioning of the whole, yet each part is different and has its distinctive role to fulfill.

3. *"One Plus One = One"*

This is divine arithmetic.
  •In Ephesians 2:14-22, Paul presents a "double reconciliation"
   between Man and God
   between Jew and Gentile
  •"The Middle Wall"—like the Berlin Wall (which segregates East from West) there used to be a stone wall built across the temple area in Jerusalem. This wall, built to a height of almost 6 feet, actually separated the area known as the "Court of the Gentiles" from the "Court of the Women." No Gentile could pass this barrier. A warning was inscribed at intervals along this wall stating in Hebrew, Greek, and Latin that any foreigner who trespassed beyond it would do so at pain of death. This reference would be specially significant for the Ephesians because Paul was falsely charged with the offense of "sacrilege" for having introduced Trophimus (an Ephesian and a Gentile) into this proscribed area—read Acts 21:28-29 and compare Ephesians 3:1. A similar device can be seen, even today, in many Roman Catholic and Anglican churches. It is called "the rood screen" ("rood" is an ancient name for "cross"). This screen, which separates the nave from the choir, served originally as a barrier to keep the laity from the area reserved for the clergy and choir.

Thank God all such segregating devices are nullified in Christ, whether between Jew and Gentile or "clergy" and "laity." Read Galatians 3:28.

4. *Access Guaranteed (to all)*

  •God welcomes us
  •Christ provides the way   } Ephesians 2:18
  •The Holy Spirit introduces us

5. *Appointment of Leaders*
•The Holy-Spirit-appointed leaders were a further means of strengthening the churches—see Acts 20:28 RV.

•The wisdom of such leadership prevented a threatened schism in the Jerusalem church—read Acts 6.

Note that the seven almoners or deacons, who were appointed to deal with the problem, were Hellenistic Jews (judging from their names) and at least one of them, Nicolas of Antioch, was evidently a Gentile convert to Judaism. This suggests that in the early days, even before the general inclusion of Gentiles in the Church, a new Spirit, different from the exclusiveness of Judaism, was already uniting Christians together.

Study 10

SECOND BIRTHDAY GIFTS

Scripture: 1 Corinthians 12:1-31
Memory: Ephesians 4:7
Textbook: pages 86-96

Introduction
This study serves as a general introduction to the subject of spiritual gifts. The various New Testament terms are examined and classified in an attempt to discover their purpose.

1. *Universality*
Scripture clearly teaches that every believer has at least one gift. Many have more than one. See Ephesians 4:7 and 1 Corinthians 12:7.

2. *A Distinction to Be Made*
•Spiritual gifts are not the same as natural talents, although both are given by the One Sovereign and Omniscient LORD.

•Talents are ''natural'' (all men).

•Spiritual gifts are ''supernatural'' (Christians only).

•May well be complementary in a life, i.e., spiritual gift complements natural talent.

•Important to understand that spiritual gift does not necessarily complement natural talent. Only spiritual gifts edify, and then only if exercised in love (see 1 Corinthians 13). Our spirituality does not relate to the number of spiritual gifts we may posses. A person may have great gift but be "carnal" (i.e., ruled by the flesh or self). We see an example of this in the Corinthian church. (Compare 1 Corinthians 1:7 and 3:1)

3. *Terms*
   • Two key words are
   charismata (stresses the gift which finds its source in grace (*charis*)
   pneumatika (stresses the Giver and the purpose of the gift)
   These terms are practically synonymous.
   • Examine the list of less frequently used terms (9 of them noted in the text) and consider their Biblical contexts. It would be useful to use a dictionary of New Testament terms (for example: W.E. Vine's *Expository Dictionary of New Testament Words*).
   • Are there other terms describing gifts?

4. *Classification*
   • The student would derive the most benefit from making his own careful analysis of the gifts spoken about in the New Testament. The classification (textbook page 93) deals with the five passages—four from Paul and one from Peter—where gifts are dealt with.
   • Be sure to read the paragraphs immediately preceding and following this classification in the text, pages 92-95.

5. *Purpose*
   • The key purpose of the spiritual gifts is *edification* (i.e., to *build up*).
   • Gifts are not for personal prestige nor as aids for "ego-trips." They are given to members of the Body with a view to the common good—(1 Corinthians 12:7 RSV).

Study 11

TURNED ON FOR GOD / Scripture: Romans 12:1-21
Memory: Romans 12:1-2
Textbook: pages 97-104

(May be extended into 2 sessions)

There are many Christians who have a reasonable understanding of the New Testament teaching about spiritual gifts, but who still experience a degree of frustration when it comes to identifying their own gift. It is not that they are unwilling to exercise their gift but rather that they have never received much practical help in discovering it.

In this study we shall first review the highlights of chapter 10 in the textbook, then go through a work sheet which is intended as a practical guide to discovering spiritual gifts.

Question #1 (See Prerequisites, pages 97-99)

"How can I begin to discover God's will in this matter of my spiritual gift?" Here are some suggestions:

•Make sure that you really are willing to obey the Lord and yield yourself to Him (Romans 12:1-2).

•Tell the Lord that you are available—consider John 7:17.

•Seek information from the Scriptures and reliable Christian commentaries concerning spiritual gifts (1 Timothy 4:13-16).

•Get involved in Christian work however lacking in glamor the job may be (Genesis 24:27).

Question #2 (see Criteria, pages 99-102)

"What tests can I apply?"

•Desire: "Do you really have a longing to do a certain thing?"

•Enjoyment: "Do you enjoy doing it?"

•Recognition: "Have other people suggested that this is your area of gift?"

•Results: "Have you noticed that the Lord has used you in a certain way and given you fruit?"

Question #3 (see Development, pages 102-104).

"How can I develop my spiritual gift?"

•By cultivating proper attitudes, e.g., faith, patience, persistence, reliability.

•By taking action:

Getting exposure in charitable volunteer agencies.

Seek some help in the field of homiletics.

Do some work in the area of your gift, in the setting of your local church.

The following work sheets have been designed to help anyone who has a genuine desire to serve the Lord in the fellowship of His Body, the Church. Obviously we must approach this subject with care and prayer. This is not intended as a do-it-yourself, instant-service kit. We recognize fully that in the final analysis each believer must seek the Lord's mind for his service. Unquestionably every Christian has at least one spiritual gift; some have several.

If you still are not sure what your gift is, then why not take time to go through this exercise carefully. This may prove to be a means of "stirring up your gift." First time go through without consultation.

Instructions

The following list of criteria statements is intended to help you identify your spiritual gift. It is by no means exhaustive but it will get you started. This is what to do:

●First, determine that you will be scrupulously honest yet humbly courageous in your answers.

●Deal with one criteria statement at a time.

●Read each statement carefully and think about it before writing down anything.

●Go through the entire list but write answers in Column 1 (*right hand side*) *only*. The idea here is to match a New Testament gift against each criteria statement.

●Having completed Column 1 (New Testament Gifts), cover that column so that it is out of sight (no peeping!). Now set your list aside until the next day.

●Keep Column 1 covered and prepare to go through the list again. This time read each criteria statement through and see if it describes you.

●Assess yourself as follows:

If the statement describes you or you would really like it to, then write A opposite the statement, under Column 2 (Personal Inclination).

If you are inclined toward this, write B in Column 2.

If you are not sure—write C.

If this definitely is not "your thing" write D.

●Now, having completed both columns independently of each other, uncover Column 1 so that you can read the columns together.

●Notice prayerfully where your A's match up with a New Testament spiritual gift. This should give you a start in identifying your gift. Now feel free to consult a mature fellow Christian.

Example

Criteria Statement	*Column 2*	*Column 1*
Enjoys caring for the sick and deprived	A	Showing Mercy

First time through, do this without consultation

		New
	Personal	*Testament*
	Inclination	*Gifts*
CRITERIA STATEMENTS	Column 2	Column 1

1. Likes to spend a lot of time and energy counseling people. _____ _____
2. Has a good library of Bible helps, enjoys study. _____ _____

30

3. Always happy to assist in cleanup after a fellowship meal. _____ _____
4. Enjoys working behind the scenes to insure the success of a program. _____ _____
5. Others see him/her as a person of vision. _____ _____
6. He/She is happy to organize registration and accommodations for a camp, retreat, etc. _____ _____
7. Encourages other Christians in specific areas of their lives. _____ _____
8. Finds great joy in giving of funds and possessions. _____ _____
9. Has a special sympathy/empathy for retarded, handicapped, and underprivileged folk. _____ _____
10. Happy to see or hear of men and women coming to a personal and saving knowledge of Jesus Christ. _____ _____
11. Always on the lookout for the neglected and lonely members, with the intent to show them love and concern. _____ _____
12. By prayer, counsel, understanding, always trying to win back the backslider. _____ _____
13. Will gladly take care of other people's children so the latter can go and counsel a week at camp, etc. _____ _____
14. Has a consistent care for the church building and grounds. _____ _____
15. Willing and happy to give well beyond a culturally/socially acceptable minimum. _____ _____
16. Often thinking of different ways to teach various Scripture truths and eager to try them out. _____ _____
17. Happily gives time, energy, and/or money in showing compassion to the aged and the ill. _____ _____
18. Often encouraging the saints, individually or corporately, in the need of personal evangelism. _____ _____
19. Directing a week at camp is an exciting challenge. _____ _____
20. His admonitions usually bring hoped-for improvement and change. _____ _____
21. He/She dreams "dreams for God"—and attempts to put some into reality—a new venture, program, etc. _____ _____
22. Regular visitation of the saints is part of his/her life style. _____ _____
23. Spends time in encouraging and teaching men and women to be shepherds. _____ _____
24. Has keen interest in the study of the Scriptures. _____ _____
25. Enjoys ushering, taping messages, and taking care of the emblems for the Lord's Supper. _____ _____
26. Very alert to the financial needs of God's men/women, work. _____ _____
27. Often moved to offer a word of encouragement to a saint who is a little "down in the mouth." _____ _____
28. His response is positive when asked by the deacons to head up the social committee for the year. _____ _____

29. Often the shut-in, the suffering, are a major focus of his prayers.

30. He seems more inclined towards reaching the lost than teaching the saints.

31. His great concern is that young Christians grow in the Word.

32. Often asked to lead a Bible study (and enjoys it).

33. Obstacles to a promising idea (the barriers)—financial, individual, or traditional—do not deter him permanently from trying to realize the idea.

34. He/She often feels drawn toward those who are suffering—physically, mentally, spiritually—and more than a feeling of pity, he acts.

35. He/She is happy to use typing skills and to cut stencils.

36. He/She seeks to be open to help meet material needs of the saints.

37. He/She has both a very clear understanding of the gospel message and has been successful in a clear communication of the same.

38. He digs deeper into the Word as he sees the church lacking in certain areas.

39. Willingly picks up children regularly for Sunday school and/or the elderly for church services.

40. Finds joy in playing the piano/organ for church services, Sunday school, clubs, camp, etc.

41. William Carey's quote: "Attempt great things for God, expect great things from God"—is one he would like to adopt for the rest of his years.

42. Able to effectively share his/her vision, ideas, and goals and motivate others to follow.

43. Quick to console the depressed, perhaps phoning or writing in a Spirit-led spur of the moment.

44. Upon hearing of a sick Christian and/or neighbor, she moves to cook a meal, run errands, or do whatever is necessary.

45. He is really burdened about his unsaved neighbors, colleagues, etc., always alert to opportunities to share Christ.

46. Concerned about protecting the saints from false doctrine and false teachers.

47. Is confident (in the Lord) and competent in leading a Sunday school class.

48. Has keen awareness of being a godly example to the believers around him.

49. Is willing to use his/her bookkeeping experience to help in the church's finances.

50. Often on his mind and in his prayer requests are possible opportunities to give where most urgently needed.

51. Emboldened to urge a believer to "go on for the Lord," possibly suggesting creative ways to exercise gift more effectively.	_____ _____
52. Has a burden to train other Christians in methodology and message regarding reaching the unsaved.	_____ _____
53. Accepts responsibility of communicating Bible truths with delight and a feeling of challenge and anticipation.	_____ _____
54. She runs the nursery month after month to free mothers to attend class.	_____ _____
55. Enjoys entertaining people in her home.	_____ _____
56. Never happier than when fixing things for people.	_____ _____
57. Has a real gift with words and holds an audience.	_____ _____
58. Seems to see through to the core of a problem.	_____ _____
59. Finds fulfillment in administration.	_____ _____
60. Has a good analytical mind.	_____ _____

Study 12

GETTING THINGS IN PERSPECTIVE

Scripture: Ephesians 4:1-16
Memory: 1 Peter 4:10
Textbook: pages 105-128

Here we are concerned with a more detailed understanding of the gifts. This study will follow the general analysis of the gifts as outlined in the textbook chapters 11, 12, and 13. These chapters should be read over carefully.

1. *Gifts for Oral Ministry* (speaking)
    •*Prophecy*
    An important foundational gift in the early church.
    A medium for the communication of truth before the completion of the canon of Scripture.
    Required strict regulation because liable to abuse.
    "Telling forth" rather than "foretelling."
    •*Apostle*
    Another foundation gift (Ephesians 2:20); read footnote on page 109.

    The criteria of apostleship preclude all but first-generation Christians (Acts 1:22 and 1 Corinthians 9:1 ff.)

Beware of overstating the idea that present-day Christians are apostles in a secondary sense. This tends to create an elitist group within churches. (There are plenty of people who would like us to believe they are apostles—for obvious reasons!)

• *Teaching*

An ongoing task and extremely necessary in every generation.

A gift that can be sharpened through the disciplined application of the mind to the Scriptures.

• *Exhortation*

Consider the two interpretations of *paraklēsis*.

• *Evangelist*

Essentially a herald of good news. May be exercised publicly or privately.

• *Word of Knowledge—Wisdom*

Probably another precanon medium of revelation.

2. *Gifts for practical service*

These gifts being less glamorous and less visible may be neglected. However they are equally important.

• *Administration*

These gifts relate to church government and leadership.

(See "Government," page 114 and "He That Ruleth," page 115.)

The New Testament lays considerable emphasis on Christian leadership. It stresses the charismatic (i.e., relating to gift), personal, social, conjugal, and domestic qualifications of leaders. (For a fuller discussion of this subject see the author's *Living Churches*, Paternoster, England, 1972.)

• *Missions of Mercy*

While all believers are called to the exercise of Christian kindness some are specially equipped.

Special words include: service, generosity, showing mercy, helps.

• *Faith*

Probably something different from the "faith" by which all Christians must walk.

• *Hospitality*

To be shown by all but done particularly well by some.

Hospitality does not need to be lavish, just genuine.

• *Miraculous Manifestations*

These gifts are probably best viewed as essentially first generation phenomena. Certainly there can be some contemporary application of the principles involved here. God is still the God of miracles but Scripture is economical in its emphasis on the miraculous. It says of the greatest man who ever lived, John Baptist, "John did no miracle: but all things that John spake of this man were true" (John 10:41).

Of some modern media preachers it could be said: "All they try to do is miracles and many of the things they say about the Scriptures are untrue."

• *Gifts of healings* (see pages 123-125) (A useful recent booklet,

Healing—Examined by a Doctor, by Dr. Arthur Hill. Everyday Publications.)
- *Working of miracles* (see page 126)
- *Discerning of Spirits* (see pages 126-128)

Study 13

TRUTH OR TRIP?

Scripture: Isaiah 28:9-16
Memory: Psalm 119:89
Textbook: pages 129-134

Introduction to Studies 13—20

We have considered the Spirit's ministry in relation to the corporate life of the Church—the Body. Now we turn to those special and personal ministries of the Spirit in the life and experience of the individual Christian. Each of the next 7 studies could be developed into a complete book study but we must content ourselves with some basic and introductory concepts. Hopefully, in dealing with these more intimate aspects of the Spirit's work, our studies will lead us into a deeper devotion to the Lord Jesus, not simply into a better understanding of pneumatology.

Study 13 is brief but important because it deals with the recurring question: ''By what authority?''

Here the author insists that Scripture is our final, peerless authority. No matter how impressive, experience must always bow to and be tested by the criteria set forth in the absolute revelation of Scripture.

The Key Points of this Chapter

- While desire for revival is commendable we must always recognize that zeal without knowledge is fanaticism.

- Since the same Holy Spirit who inspired Scripture indwells the believer, His revelation in Scripture and His work in our lives will be absolutely consistent, never causing confusion.

- It is essential to strike a balance between the careful systematic study of God's Word and emotional experience.

- Spiritual growth and maturity result from our knowledge of and obedience to Scripture, not from strange mystical or emotional ''trips.''

35

•Even mountaintop experiences are inconsequential compared to the bedrock inspired revelations of Scripture—ask Peter! (2 Peter 1:19)

•Scripture must be judiciously expounded and properly understood. Hermeneutics are basic.

•Distinguish always between the historical (narrative) and the doctrinal (didactic) parts of Scripture.

Study 14

GOD'S FOREVER FAMILY

Scripture: John 3:1-21
Memory: John 3:5
Textbook: pages 135-139

Introduction
While the terms regeneration and adoption are closely associated, they describe different truths in relation to our place in "God's forever family." We are both born into and adopted into this family!

1. *Regeneration*
The Holy Spirit was not only the divine instrument in creation but in recreation. In this connection we usually describe our new beginning as regeneration. The popular term is new birth or being born again. In the term, born again, the word "again" translates *anōthen*, which can also be translated "anew" or "from above."
(For a clearer understanding of this subject in context read our Lord's conversation with Nicodemus in John 3.)
•*John 3*—key phrases:
Born of water and the Spirit—possible references:
    Physical birth contrasted with spiritual birth (cf., John 1:13)
    Water refers to the Word of God (Ephesians 5:26)
    Water refers to John Baptist's "baptism unto repentance"
    The phrase could translate "born of water, i.e., the Spirit"
"That which is born of the Spirit"—this phrase stresses:
    The absolute contrast between flesh and spirit
    The impotence of man as spiritually *dead*
    The glorious power of the Holy Spirit to effect spiritual life in the believing heart

36

INSTRUCTIONS FOR USE
OF VISUAL AIDS

The visuals found in the center of this study guide are professionally prepared to supplement and enhance your study. The use of visuals dramatically increases retention of studied materials, so it is hoped that you will make full use of those provided with this guide.

The visuals are so designed that they may be used in several ways. Individuals utilizing this guide on their own may use them as personal study charts just as they are found in the guide. Teachers preparing for class instruction may use them to make overhead transparencies or class handouts.

The publisher intends that these visuals be widely used. Reproduction for class use is in no way considered to be a violation of Loizeaux Brothers' copyright.

Removing Visuals

The visuals in this guide are held in by two staples. Carefully lift the tongs of the staples and lift off the visuals and these instructions. Then close up the staples so they will hold the rest of your guide together.

We suggest that you keep your visuals in a file folder along with any transparencies or handouts you make. This will keep them clean and ready for use.

To insure good reproduction flatten each visual by running a fingernail or a blunt object along the back of the crease.

Making Transparencies

The most common means of making transparencies from visuals such as those included with this guide is with a thermal copier. Special plastic film is placed on top of the visual and passed through the copier. This method is fast, and very economical.

Some other photo-type copiers can also be used to make transparencies. Check your owner's manual to see if this is possible and what type of plastic film must be used.

If you do not have a copier available which will mechanically produce a transparency, you can make one by hand by placing clear plastic film over the visual and tracing with special transparency markers.

(Continued opposite page 37)

SYMBOL	Reference
e.g. WIND	*John 3:*

:VELATION

)LY SPIRIT

IN SCRIPTURE
("Inspiration")

---

2 Timothy 3:16
2 Peter 1:21

y Loizeaux Brothers, Inc.

THE WORD

"GO

Infallible
Inerrant
Authorative
Living
Eternal
Final

" . . . is therefore
profitable for ":

Church
hurch
's Body

}

**Temples
(naoi)
of the
Holy Spirit**

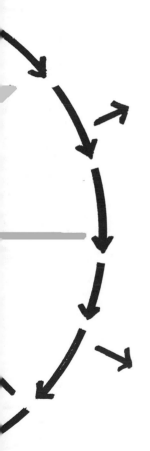

*Arrows pointing
inward =*
**Devotion
to Christ**

*Arrows pointing
outward =*
Evangelism

*Arrows around
circle =*
**Concern and
love for
each other**

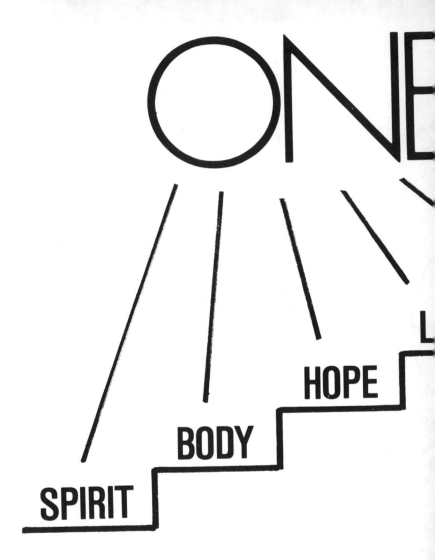

"seven unit

ONE

SPIRIT

BODY

HOPE

L

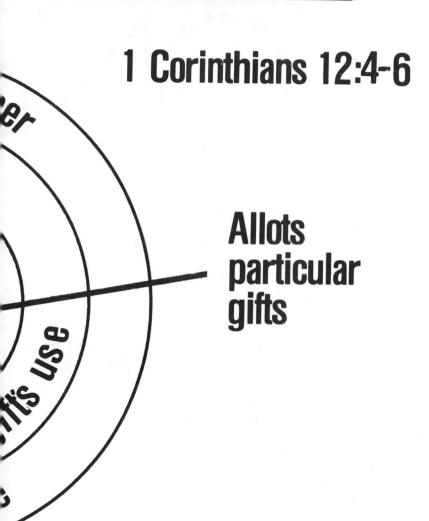

AND THE GIFTS

1 Corinthians 12:4-6

**Allots
particular
gifts**

er

fts use

Loizeaux Brothers, Inc.

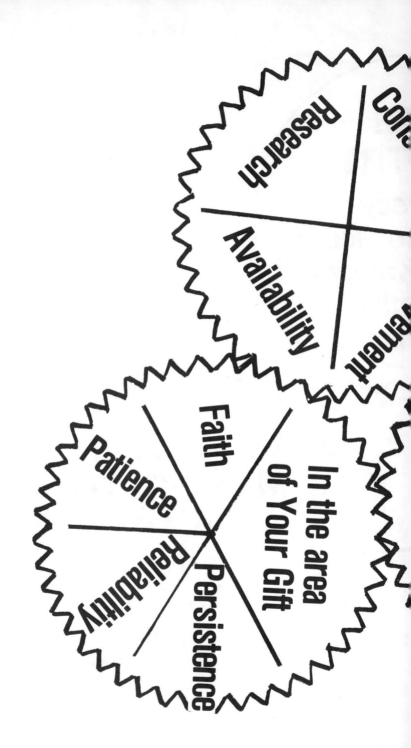

Research
Cor[...]
Availability
[...]ment

Faith
Patience
Reliability
Persistence
In the area of Your Gift

**AL
TRY**

*ecy
owledge
vangelist
ation
her*

**MIRACULOUS
MANIFESTA-
TIONS**
*Healings
Miracles
Tongues
Interpretations*

izeaux Brothers, Inc.

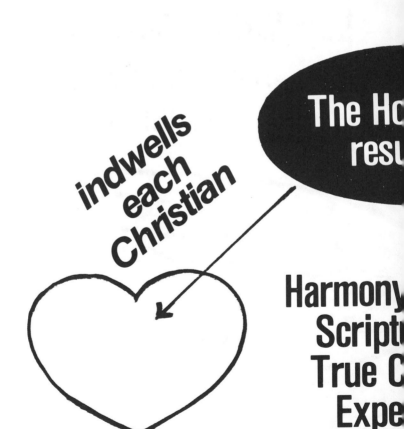

SPIRITUAL MATH
Zeal – Knowled
Knowledge – Ze
Knowledge + Zo

The Ho
resu

indwells
each
Christian

Harmony
Script
True C
Expe

REDEMPTION
"Children"

We are literally "born" into God's forever family

By the Spirit

Loizeaux Brothers, Inc.

PEN

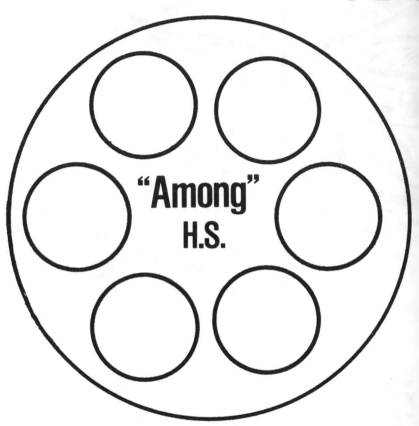

"Among"
H.S.

"For He (Holy
with (p
and shall b

SEALED

**WALKING
by the Spirit**

by Loizeaux Brothers, Inc.

WISDOM

ASSU

HOPE ←

T
HO
SP
Secre
Chri
L

LIBERTY ←

STRI

E – Ephesians 5:18

.. *i.e.= a command*

.. *i.e.= all Christians*

.. *i.e. = a continuing responsibility*

.. *i.e.= The Holy Spirit is the initiator*

LE

filled and stimulated
ly) spirit"

Loizeaux Brothers, Inc.

FRU[IT]
OF T[HE]
SPI[RIT]

INWARD
Love
Joy
Peace

SO[CIAL]
Longs[uffering]
Gentl[eness]
Goo[dness]

N.T. COMMANDS (Imperatives)

1. Be filled with the Spirit
2. Walk in the Spirit

NEGATIVES

3. Grieve not the Holy Spirit
4. Quench not the Spirit

Loizeaux Brothers, Inc.

W
BR
DO

ACCESS BY

GENTILES
"In Christ"

ONE N
ONE LORD - ONE F

INTROSPECTION
FRUSTRATION
WRONG VALUES
CONFUSION
WRONG EMPHASIS
CONCEIT
APATHY
DIVISION

oizeaux Brothers, Inc.

PENTECOST

Definite human languages (dialects)

Result: Clarification

No Interpreters

Spiritually beneficial

Speakers evidently understood

EXPERIENCE

human

unreliable

temporal

varies

firm

conflict

egarded as the criterion
rnative to Scripture.

izeaux Brothers, Inc.

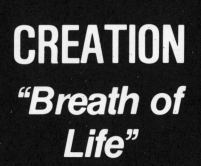

THE
SP

CREATION
"Breath of Life"

CONV
*o
righte
jud*

VISUAL FOR STUDY 25. *Study Guide, The Holy Spirit: Lord and Life-Giver.* ©

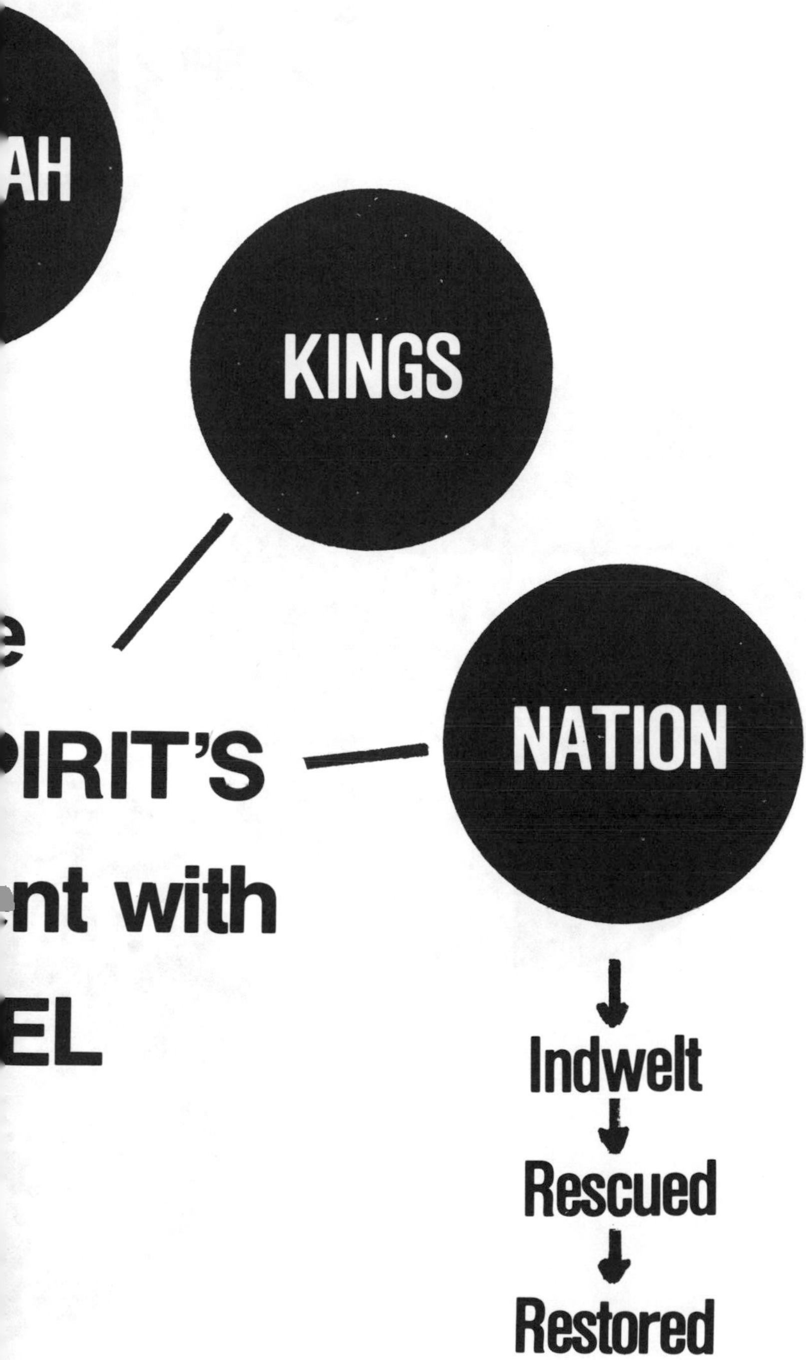

AH

KINGS

e

PIRIT'S

nt with

EL

NATION

↓
Indwelt
↓
Rescued
↓
Restored

izeaux Brothers, Inc.

SINS AGAINST

BLASPHEMY

GRIEVING

ty"

resence"

potence"

science"

MAN (by contrast) = finite
Temporal
Local
Frail
Ignorant

All predicated by the Spirit

He knows (cognition)
He feels (emotion)
He wills (volition)

Examine references

VISUAL FOR STUDY 3. *Study Guide, The Holy Spirit: Lord and Life-Giver.* © 198

1. O.T. NAMES

a. Deity

"Spirit of God"
"Spirit of the Lord"

b. Attributes

"Spirit of Wisdom"
"Spirit of Burning"

Loizeaux Brothers, Inc.

HOW TO

1. PRAYERFULLY

2. CAREFULLY ..

3. HONESTLY ....

4. BIBLICALLY ...

5. HUMBLY ....

6. PRACTICALLY

7. EXPECTANTLY

(These principles are
but especially

VISUAL FOR STUDY 1. *Study Guide, The Holy Spirit: Lord and Life-Giver.* © 198

STUDY

..... **on our knees**

..... **with listening ears**

..... **with open mind**

..... **with clear head**

..... **with pure heart**

..... **with willing hands**

..... **with a keen eye**

portant for any studies
Pneumatology)

oizeaux Brothers, Inc.

2. N.T. NAMES

In relation to the Father
e.g. "Spirit of your Father"

In relation to the Son
"Spirit of Jesus"

In relation to Scripture
"Spirit of Truth"

In relation to the Christian
"Spirit of adoption"

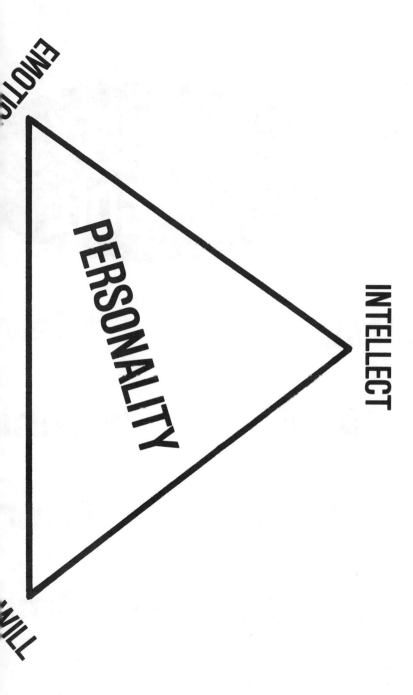

EMOTION

INTELLECT

WILL

PERSONALITY

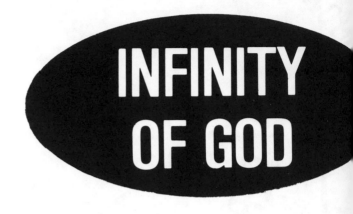

TIME . . . . "Eter

SPACE . . . . "Omni

POWER . . . . "Omr

KNOWLEDGE "Omr

VISUAL FOR STUDY 4. *Study Guide, The Holy Spirit: Lord and Life-Giver.* © 198(

Interpretation

God's Inscrutable Power

izeaux Brothers, Inc.

DIVINE R[

BY THE H

IN CHRIST
("Incarnation")
___

cf. John 1:1-18
Hebrews 1:1-3

VISUAL FOR STUDY 6. *Study Guide, The Holy Spirit: Lord and Life-Giver.* ©

OF GOD

"- BREATHED
CRIPTURE"

"Inspired by the Holy Spirit"

- Teaching
- Rebuke
- Correction
- Training

Loizeaux Brothers, Inc.

Eph. 2:21   The Univers[a]
1 Cor. 3:16   The Local
1 Cor. 6.19   The Believ[e]

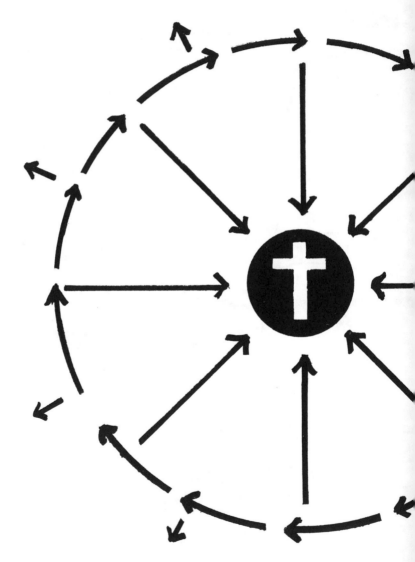

es"

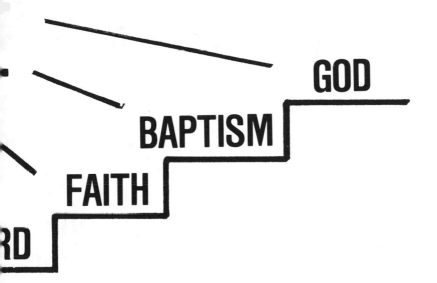

GOD

BAPTISM

FAITH

RD

oizeaux Brothers, Inc.

THE GODHEAD

From the Fa

By the So

Through
the
Holy —
Spirit

Directs sphere o

Ultimate sou

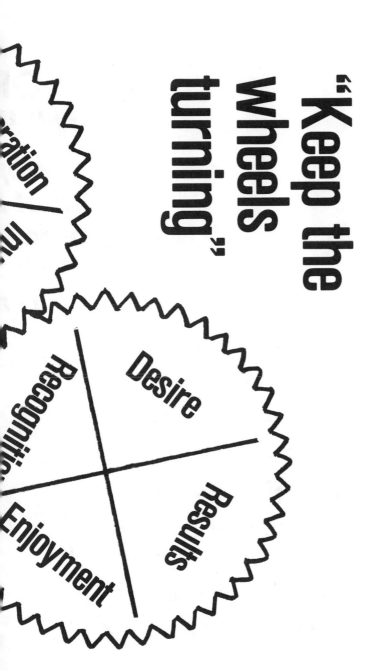

"Keep the wheels turning"

ration / En...

Desire

Recognitio...

Results

Enjoyment

izeaux Brothers, Inc.

O[...]
MIN [...]

Prop[...]
Word of [...]
Apostle - [...]
Exho[...]
Tea[...]

PRACTICAL SERVICE

Administration
Missions of Mercy
Hospitality - Service
Faith - Helps
Generosity

e = **Fanaticism**
ıl = **Orthodoxy**
al = **Maturity**

Spirit
s in

inspired
scripture

etween
and
istian
nce

izeaux Brothers, Inc.

ADOPTION
"Sons"

We are welcomed by God into His Family as Sons — granted all the privileges as heirs

ECOST

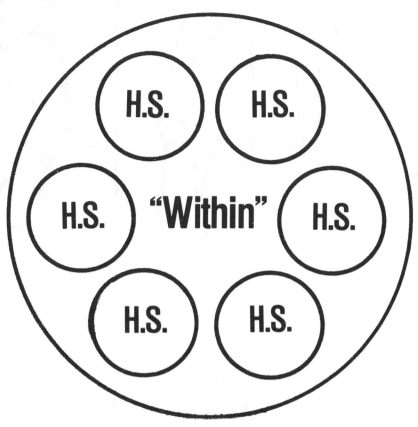

H.S. **H.S.**

H.S. **"Within"** **H.S.**

H.S. **H.S.**

pirit) **dwelleth**
a) **you**
n *(en)* **you"**
—John 14:17

Loizeaux Brothers, Inc.

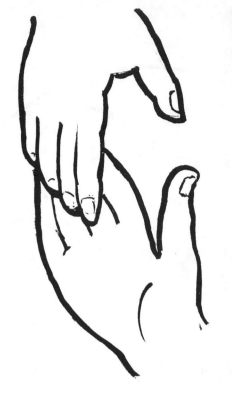

"LED BY THE SPIRIT"
God's Hand on mine

VISUAL FOR STUDY 16. *Study Guide, The Holy Spirit: Lord and Life-Giver.*

ANCE

HOLINESS

E
LY
RIT
of the
tian
e

LOVE

PRAYER

GTH

oizeaux Brothers, Inc.

PAUL'S IMPERAT

"Plērousth

1. **Imperative mooc**

2. **Plural number** ..

3. **Present tense** ...

4. **Passive voice** ...

AMPLIFIED B

"but ever
with the (

OUTWARD
Faithfulness
Meekness
Temperance

AL

ering

ness

ess

zeaux Brothers, Inc.

BUT NOWHERE!

Be baptized by the Spirit
Speak in tongues
Heal by the Spirit
Give prophetic utterances
by the Spirit

SO BEWARE!

LL
KEN
WN

ONE SPIRIT

JEWS
"In Christ"

MAN
H - ONE BAPTISM

izeaux Brothers, Inc.

VISUAL FOR STUDY 22. *Study Guide, The Holy Spirit: Lord and Life-Giver.* ©

CORINTH

Probably ecstatic utterances or dialects

Result: Confusion

Interpreters required

Indiscriminate

Unintelligible to Speaker

bizeaux Brothers, Inc.

THE WORD OF GOD

Divine

Unchanging

Eternal

Unerring

may c

or ma

Experience must never l
of Truth nor as an a

HOLY
RIT

CONVERSION
*"The Living
Word"*

CTION
*in
usness
nent*

MES

LEADERS
PRIESTS

PROPHETS — — HOLY J

T

involver

ISF

↓

Speaking

↓

Writing

LYING

QUENCHING

RESISTING

Loizeaux Brothers, Inc.

INSTRUCTIONS FOR USE
OF VISUAL AIDS

(Continued from opposite page 36)

Making Class Handouts

A thermal copier can also be used to make ditto or mimeograph masters from these visuals. Again, special stencils must be used. Consult your owner's manual for complete instructions.

A Final Note

For a more complete discussion of the making of transparencies and general use of the overhead projector we suggest that you obtain *How To Make and Use Overhead Transparencies* by Anna Sue Darkes, published by Moody Press. This book, as well as overhead projectors and supplies, may well be available at your local Christian bookstore. If they are not, we suggest that you write to: Faith Venture Visuals, Post Office Box 423, Lititz, Pennsylvania 17543.

•*Titus 3:5*—important items to note:

Regeneration (Greek, *palingenesia*, derived from the roots *palin*, again and *genesis*, birth or origin). This is one of two places in the New Testament where this word is used and only here with this connotation. (The other occurrence in Matthew 19:28 relates to what Moulton and Milligan call "the Messianic rebirth of the world" *Vocabulary of the Greek Testament*, page 476; cf., Amplified Version).

Washing (Greek, *loutron*)—This word can mean washing, bath, or laver (see Ephesians 5:26 for the only other New Testament reference). Clearly the Apostle Paul is using this word metaphorically, not literally. This has nothing to do with any form of water baptism. It relates to our being made completely new. (Renewing, Greek, *anakainōseōs*—the idea here is of our being totally renewed, regenerated, not just repaired or refurbished, cf., 2 Corinthians 5:17.) As the Lord Jesus pours out the Holy Spirit upon us when we trust in Him.

•*1 Peter 1:21-23*

Note, the Trinity is involved in new birth:

God the Father is its source
God the Son pays the price (Redeemer)
God the Spirit leads us to obey the truth
Note the importance of the Eternal Word

2. *Adoption*

The English word adoption translates the Greek word *huiothesia*, which in turn is derived from the roots, *huios*, a son, and *tithēmi*, to place.

There are three passages where it is used which relate to this study:

Romans 8:15-16
Galatians 4:5-6
Ephesians 1:5

While regeneration relates to our being born into God's family, adoption has to do with our status in God's family as sons and heirs. We are placed as sons in God's family.

The Holy Spirit not only effects this miracle in relation to our "standing" before God but confirms it experientially in our hearts.

Note on Adoption

The word adoption is used by Paul alone of New Testament writers, and by him 5 times; the other occurrences are Romans 8:15,23; 9:4; Galatians 4:5. "Adoption seemed to be the most comprehensive concept that Paul employed of man's restoration. Adoption involves a crisis in the life of the believers followed by a process and it points to an eschatological completion. The ultimate purpose of adoption is the restoration of man to freedom and to harmonious relationship with God his Father" (F.F. Bruce: *Epistle to Ephesians*, Pickering and Inglis, page 29, footnote).

GLIDING OR FLYING

Scripture: Galatians 3:1-14
Memory: John 14:16-17
Textbook: pages 140-144

Keynote

All true believers in Our Lord Jesus Christ are indwelt by God the Holy Spirit. This lesson will underline that fact.

1. *A Stimulating Promise*

Jesus suggests (see John 14:16-17) that, whereas the Holy Spirit's presence has been enjoyed by the disciples as a group, the time is imminent (Pentecost) when each of them will experience the Spirit's presence within him!

2. *A Divine Necessity*—Romans 8:9

•It is impossible to be a Christian apart from the indwelling Holy Spirit.
•It is because he is indwelt that the Christian can be set free. ("Spirit of Christ" = The Holy Spirit)

Beware of the following *FALSE* Statements:
    A Christian must seek and pray to receive the Holy Spirit
    A Christian needs to experience a "second blessing"
    Only some Christians have the Holy Spirit
    A Christian can lose the Holy Spirit
(All these statements are based on erroneous, non-Biblical teaching!) List others.

3. *A Purchased Possession*—1 Corinthians 6:19

"A Christian's body is the temple of the Holy Spirit." This statement by Paul implies:
•The Christian's body is sacred (beware of pollution).
•The Christian's body as well as his spirit are of great significance and part of God's eternal purpose.
•Since Paul tells the "carnal" Corinthians this, it is evident he believed that *all* (not just a special group) are indwelt.

4. *A Wonderful Future*—Romans 8:11

What a hope!

It is important to understand that the Christian view of the body (our physical part) is so opposite to the pagan view. The ancient Greeks regarded the body as a sort of "prison house of the soul," something inferior and loathsome. This led to two extremes:

•On the one hand they said, "indulge your fleshly appetites, after all, the Spirit alone is important." That view is called "libertinism" (i.e., modern "free love").

•On the other hand this inadequate view of the body led to another extreme which said, "Curb all appetites of the body and subdue all desire. Cultivate the Spirit alone." This view is called "asceticism."

The Christian is certainly called to control his fleshly appetites but not to a morbid denial of the body. After all, God took a real, physical body in the Incarnation. When Jesus rose again His body (actual, real, tangible, etc.) was involved. His resurrection guarantees ours. This means that our body (actual, real, tangible, etc.) has a glorious future.

How is this guaranteed? By the present indwelling in our mortal bodies of the gracious Holy Spirit.

5. A Proper Perspective—Galatians 3:2-7

Here Paul is answering the insidious "doctrine of merit" being propagated by the Judaizers in Galatia. His keynote is "by *grace alone.*" His argument hinges on the fact that when a person becomes a Christian, that is, "beginning in the Spirit," he says you go on as you began, that is, *in the Spirit.* Again he is implying that *all* Christians have the Spirit.

6. An Undeserved Gift—1 John 2:20; 4:13

•For John (as for Paul) the Holy Spirit is the hallmark of the Christian. A gift is a gift

not a reward

not a recognition of achievement

not the result of good works, prayers, etc.

How strange that some Christians who insist that salvation is God's gift (nothing to do with works) say that God's gift of the Spirit must be sought, prayed for, waited for, etc.

The Spirit is given without distinction to all—read Paul's magnificent words in Ephesians 1:3: *all spiritual blessings.*

Study 16

GOD'S HAND ON MINE

Scripture: Romans 8:1-17,26-27
Memory: Ephesians 1:13
Textbook: pages 145-149

Introduction

The presence of the Holy Spirit in the believer's life is the proof of his sonship. The Spirit is the family hallmark. Not only is the Christian "sealed" and "led" by the Spirit, he also walks by the Spirit.

1. *Sealed by the Spirit* (textbook pages 145-147)
•In Bible times a well-loved slave might be adopted into his master's family to become his son and heir.

•This adoption would sometimes be "sealed" by a ring. It was the mark of sonship. (See the story of the prodigal son—Luke 15:22.)

• As Christians (i.e., people who have believed) we receive the Holy Spirit as the seal of our sonship (see Ephesians 1:13; Galatians 4:5-6).

The believing, regeneration, and sealing are simultaneous (not sequential). (See discussion, textbook pages 145-147.)

•The seal of sonship also has a future reference. It guarantees our redemption. As "sealed sons" we shall arrive safe home.

2. *Walking by the Spirit*
•In the New Testament the word "walk" is used metaphorically of the believer's conduct.

•We have a choice—our conduct is either subject to God's will as revealed in Scripture or according to our selfish desires.

• A son will live in accordance with the best traditions of the family.

•This metaphor reminds us:
The Christian life is to be progressive.
We can depend on God's daily dynamic, His Holy Spirit.
We are called to surrender daily to the indwelling Holy Spirit.

3. *Led by the Spirit*
•Romans 8:14 (quote)
•Galatians 5:18 (quote)
•God's sons are not only directed but sustained by the Holy Spirit.
•The leading is like the hand of the parent supporting and directing the hand of the child.
•This leadership means freedom.
•The Spirit's leading will normally be through Scripture, not emotions, cf., John 10:3-5 (quote).

FREE AT LAST

Scripture: 1 Corinthians 2:1-15
Memory: Romans 8:2-3
Textbook: pages 150-159

Introduction
This study is concerned with a variety of subjects, such as:

Assurance	Prayer
Sanctification	Liberty
Wisdom	Love
Strength	Hope

These matters are brought together here because to a greater or lesser degree they all relate to the Christian's daily experience of the Holy Spirit.

In several of these studies "experience" has been played down because of the contemporary tendency to subjectivism. Here we must strike a balance. Certainly the Spirit is a part of every believer's daily experience—or should be! However, this experience is not ephemeral emotion but a sense of deep, abiding, practical, divine help.

1. *Assurance*
•The emphasis here is on the confirmatory ministry of the Holy Spirit in the heart of the believer.

•The Holy Spirit offers the objective witness of His presence in Scripture and in the Incarnation and the subjective witness of His presence in the believer's heart.

•Consider carefully:
1 John 5:7-10 (see verse 13)
Romans 8:16-17 (cf., Galatians 4:4-6)

2. *Sanctification*
•There are two aspects of sanctification:
God's—i.e., Consecration ⎱
Man's—i.e., Purification ⎰ Both by the Holy Spirit

•The Christian is "set apart" for God (as God's special possession) by the Holy Spirit—1 Peter 1:2; 2 Thessalonians 2:13; 1 Corinthians 6:11.
•He is to express this in his life:
by submission to the Holy Spirit in the Word
by setting his affection on Christ
by renouncing the old life of sin

3. *Wisdom*
•The Holy Spirit is the communicator of spiritual truth to the Christian.

•The knowledge of God is not the result of intellectual acumen but of spiritual anointing. Read:
  1 Corinthians 2:13-14
  John 16:13
  1 John 2:20,27
  cf., James 3:14-18
•The believer must, however, *apply* his regenerate mind to understand divine truth:
  1 Corinthians 14:20—in understanding be *adult*
  Colossians 3:2—literally, think heavenly things
  2 Timothy 2:15—be diligent, etc.
•Scripture warns against the "quiescent mind" approach—1 Corinthians 14:14-15.

4. Strength
•Here the emphasis is on the inner dynamic of the Holy Spirit.
•The Spirit gives:
  power for witness
  power for living
  power to conquer sin
  power to serve
•Read Acts 1:8; Ephesians 3:16; Ephesians 3:20; Philippians 1:19 (cf., 4:13).

5. Prayer
•The Holy Spirit supports and directs our prayer life. He prays "through" and "for" the believer.
•The Holy Spirit is the great intercessor. (See Study 1 re the Holy Spirit as the *Paraclete*)
•The Spirit understands both God's will and our needs. (An unbeatable combination!)

6. Liberty
•The Old Covenant (the "letter") tended to frustration because the Law revealed man's impotence to live in accordance with divine requirements. Man discovered himself to be enslaved, "sold under sin" (Romans 7:14).
•The New Covenant (the "Spirit") brings freedom because the Holy Spirit sets us free to do the will of God—Romans 8:3; Galatians 4:4; Galatians 5:1.
•No longer *slaves* but *sons*—Galatians 4.

7. Love
•The Holy Spirit floods our lives with God's love—Romans 5:5.
•The fruit of the Spirit is love (Galatians 5:22-23). All the others ("fruits") are aspects of that love.

8. Hope
•In a world of despair the Holy Spirit helps a Christian to abound in hope (Romans 15:13).
•As the One who seals us unto redemption (Ephesians 1:13) the Holy Spirit helps us live in the anticipation of that glorious day!

Study 18

OVERFLOWING / Scripture: Ephesians 5:1-21
Memory: Ephesians 5:17-18
Textbook: pages 160-166

Key Verse—Ephesians 5:18

Introduction
We must carefully define our terms and distinguish things that are different.
For example:
•Baptism in the Holy Spirit
  initiatory and once for all
•Filling of the Holy Spirit
  continuous and needs to be maintained
•One baptism, many fillings

1. A Divine Imperative
In summary we may say that Paul teaches that to be continually filled with the Holy Spirit is God's plan for every Christian as well as every Christian's responsibility.

2. Self Control, Not Abandon
Note that Paul is not *comparing* "drunkenness" with "spiritual fullness" (as some suggest on the basis of the critics' words in Acts 2:13). He is *contrasting* these experiences.
•The idea that abandonment of self-control is desirable or even an evidence of being under the influence of the Spirit is contrary to Paul's understanding.
•Self-control is a mark of the Spirit (see Galatians 5:23 and 1 Corinthians 14:32).

43

3. *What Are the Criteria?*

Paul tells us what some of the practical results of the fullness of the Holy Spirit are:

•*Fellowship*

Christians who are filled with the Spirit will at least be on speaking terms with their fellow Christians.

The "speaking" in this context is more than "talking about the weather." It will include spiritual, congregational worship—as well as singing.

•*Praise*

This suggests actual melody-making but goes beyond it to include the praise of living daily for the Lord.

> Not for the lip of praise alone
> Or e'en the praising heart
> I ask, but for a life made up
> Of praise in every part.

•*Thanksgiving*

Paul certainly suggests a high level of spiritual living when he suggests "giving thanks every day for everything." This denotes a genuinely spiritual perspective.

•*Courteous*

Far from the ostentation associated by some with "being filled with the Spirit," Paul says the mark of the Spirit-filled man is courtesy. He will be characterized by submission rather than exhibitionism.

4. *Cluttered or Clean?*

The choice between a life of barren defeat or one of fruitfulness lies with the individual Christian.

A command can be obeyed or refused.

The How To

How can we be filled with the Holy Spirit?

While we must beware of easy, three-step formulae for "*instant spirituality*" we must try to be practical.

1. Own up to all known sin.
2. Open up all the "doors" of your life to the Lord (no "keep out" signs).
3. Invite the Lord Jesus to occupy the throne.
4. Step out in the path of faith and obedience.
5. Believe God's Word.
6. Tell others about the Lord Jesus.
7. Get involved in using your "gift" in the Church.

BE FRUITFUL AND MULTIPLY

Scripture: John 15:1-17
Memory: Galatians 5:22-23
Textbook: pages 167-174

Introduction

In this study we focus attention on the famous words of the Apostle Paul in Galatians 5 about the *fruit of the Spirit* in contrast to the *works of the flesh*.

It bears repetition: As far as the Christian Life is concerned: "Miraculous phenomena there need not be, but moral virtue there must be." Beware of reversing this!

1. *An Established Metaphor*

The picture of a tree bearing fruit is well known in Scripture:

Isaiah 5:1-7—Israel, the fruitless vine
Matthew 7:20—the fruit "reveals" the tree
John 15:1-11—Jesus the True Vine

2. *Inward Virtues*

•*Love*

Note that Paul does not say "the fruits of the Spirit *are*," but uses the singular number, "the fruit of the Spirit *is*."

The love of which Paul writes here is God's love, *agapē* (cf., Romans 5:5).

List the distinctives of God's love—e.g., causeless, eternal, sacrificial, universal, etc.

•*Joy*

Here is love "rejoicing" in spite of circumstances (even adverse ones). It is significant that it is in a prison Epistle—Philippians—that Paul writes so much about "joy."

Do not confuse spiritual joy with laughing exuberance.

•*Peace*

The Bible word for "peace"—*eirēnē*—conveys the thought of wholeness. Aspects of peace:

Peace with God—through the cross work of Jesus
Peace of God—the gift of the Father
Peace through God—the fruit of the Spirit

3. *Manward (Social) Virtues*

•*Longsuffering*

The idea of this beautiful word is "patience with people." It might literally be translated "long tempered." This virtue was most beautifully displayed in our Lord's life (see Isaiah 53:7).

Consider how this Christian virtue might work in churches.
Read the note from Hogg and Vine in textbook, pages 170-171.
•*Gentleness*
Here is the basis of Christian courtesy.
Reflects the truth expressed in 1 Corinthians 13:5.
Suggests a maturity which can react graciously.
•*Goodness*
Probably better translated "benevolence." It is goodness in action—not simply an abstract, unseen virtue. Consider ways in which this fruit could be manifest.

4. *Outward Virtues*
•*Faithfulness*
This is the same word usually translated "faith." In this context it seems to mean reliability.
List some ways in which this virtue would evidence itself in a Christian's life.
Examine various translations.
•*Meekness*
This is a strong word describing that quality of humility which commands respect.
Two Bible characters who were meek, were Moses (Numbers 12:3) and Jesus (Matthew 11:29).
Prautēs suggests a balance or the mean between assertiveness and undue modesty (see Vine, *Dictionary of New Testament Words*).
•*Temperance*
This word is not really related to a person's attitude to alcohol but more to the development of control over temper and tongue. Clearly this is a fruit of the Spirit, not "the flesh."

5. *Lessons*
•These fruits are supernatural, not the result of human effort.
•We are responsible farmers who must cultivate these fruits.
•The believer still has a choice whether he will "sow" to the flesh or the Spirit.
•Jesus teaches (John 15) that only if we abide (i.e., obey) can we *bear* (not produce!) fruit.
•Without *Him* we can do nothing.

BAPTIZED
IN FIRE

/ Scripture: John 1:19-34
Memory: 1 Corinthians 12:13 RV
Textbook: pages 175-188

Introduction
In the next five Studies we deal with some of the serious misun-
derstandings of Scripture which have given rise to the extreme teachings of
the Pentecostal and charismatic movements. As we study this section we
must guard against harsh dogmatism. While we resist the temptation to
judge people, yet at the same time we must face up to the truth as revealed
in Scripture. We do the Lord and His Church a great disservice by "woolly
thinking" and by compromising with what is clearly wrong teaching, no
matter how commendable are its exponents. Excitement, activity, and noise
are not criteria of spirituality. There is much in the old proverb, "Empty
vessels make the most noise"!
One of the key phrases of the modern charismatic movement is: "the
baptism of the Holy Spirit." This experience is sought, prayed for, and
regarded as the sine qua non for the Christian who really wants to arrive. In
this study we examine what Scripture says about this concept.

1. *New Testament Teaching*
The expression "baptized in the Holy Spirit" (*en pneumati hagiō*—
literally, in Holy Spirit) occurs seven times in the New Testament.
  Matthew 3:11
  Mark 1:8
  Luke 3:16
  John 1:33
  Acts 1:5
  Acts 11:15-16
  1 Corinthians 12:13
In the first six of these passages the reference is to John the Baptizer.
A contrast is drawn between John's baptizing people in water and our
Lord's baptizing people in (the) Holy Spirit.
These six passages view the event (baptism in the Holy Spirit) as future, in
relation to John's baptism.
In Acts 1:5 our Lord says the event is imminent ("not many days hence").
In the final passage—1 Corinthians 12:13—Paul, using the past (aorist)
tense, regards it as history.

Conclusion
Whatever is meant by the expression, "baptized in the Holy Spirit," the
evidence of the New Testament is that it took place a few days after

Ascension Day and before Paul's Corinthian correspondence. Plainly, the reference is to the Day of Pentecost.

2. *"Baptism in the Holy Spirit"*
A careful examination of this key phrase reveals:
- The Scripture knows nothing of this popular contemporary expression: "the baptism *of* the Holy Spirit," which suggests that the Holy Spirit is the baptizer.
- This is not a quibble about phraseology. It is a matter of accuracy in translating Paul's words. He writes: "We were all baptized in one spirit into one body" (see textbook for a discussion of the Greek prepositions here).
- The Holy Spirit is the element into which we were immersed by Jesus when we were incorporated into His mystical Body, the Church.
- A secondary reference is clearly implied in the apostle's words as read in context.

Primary reference is to Pentecost.

Secondary reference is to each Christian's conversion, when he personally appropriates the blessing and is "joined to" the Body of Christ.

3. *Distinction Between Water Baptism and Spirit Baptism*
- When a person becomes a Christian he signifies this renewal by being immersed in water. The water baptism is the outward sign of the baptism in the Spirit.
- Water baptism is not the same as baptism in the Spirit.
- Water baptism is not essential for salvation, baptism in the Spirit is.
- While men baptize us in water only Christ baptizes us in the Spirit.
- Remission of sins and receiving of the Holy Spirit are not results of water baptism, they are both symbolized by it.

(Consult textbook for more careful discussion).

4. *Characteristics of Baptism in the Spirit*
- *It Is Universal* (1 Corinthians 12:13; Acts 2:38).

  Note the word *all* (even carnal Corinthians!)

  Spirituality is not a prerequisite for Spirit baptism, nor a result of it.

  It is impossible to be a Christian (whether carnal or spiritual) and not be baptized in the Spirit.

  All who repent (in the proper sense of this word) receive the gift of the Holy Spirit.

  (Beware of any elitist doctrine which teaches otherwise!)
- *It Is Initiatory* (see quotations on pages 185-187).

  It took place historically on the Day of Pentecost—the "birthday of the Church."

  It takes place experientially (i.e., in the experience of each Christian) at conversion—on his new birthday.

• *It Is Corporate*
The thought of Scripture is not of individuals being baptized in the Spirit but rather of the "many" being united as one. Hence we are nowhere commanded to "seek" this baptism. It is Christ's sovereign work as He incorporates the Body.

Study 21

BREAK DOWN THE WALL

Scripture: Acts 10:34-48
Memory: Acts 10:38
Textbook: pages 189-198

In this study we must examine certain scriptural passages which are alleged to teach that "baptism in the Spirit" is a distinct, postconversion experience.

1. *Day of Pentecost*—Acts 2:1-4
Question
Does the experience of the 120 disciples teach that receiving the Holy Spirit is a separate and subsequent experience to conversion?
Answer
No.
Reasons
•Pentecost was unique
•The 120 lived both before and after the Pentecost advent of the Spirit.
•The 120 represent a unique community. They lived under both the Old and the New Covenants. Their experience was unusual and atypical.
•The experience of the 3,000 converts at Pentecost should be regarded as normative. They repented (as the gospel was preached, under the inspiration of the Spirit), they received the Holy Spirit. (Note: there is not the slightest inference that any of them spoke in tongues).

2. *The Samaritan Pentecost*—Acts 8:1-17
Again we are dealing with a unique event and it is unwise to make it a pattern. It is unique for the following reasons:
•This is the first preaching of the gospel outside the Jerusalem/Judea context.
•The subjects here are the despised Samaritans.
•The apostles from Jerusalem recognized God was working in Samaria

(incredible as that seemed) but that the converts had not received the Holy Spirit, which for them seemed strange.

•The unusual step of the imposition of the apostles' hands was a visible bridging of an "unbridgeable chasm." In Christ all would be one (Jews and Samaritans).

•These events are deliberately abnormal, to help overcome prejudice.

3. *Cornelius' Home*—Acts 10:44-48

The space devoted to this story in Acts (10:1-48; 11:1-18; 15:7-11) suggests this is an epoch-making event. It is recorded for its unusualness, and carefully detailed.

The order:
•Peter's sermon
•The Holy Spirit poured out
•The Jewish visitors amazed
•Glossolalia ("magnifying God")
•Water baptism

Note the deliberate comparison between this event and the Day of Pentecost (Acts 10:47; 11:15).

This is a unique occasion (not typical) because for the first time the Holy Spirit is marking the Gentiles as belonging to the Body of Christ as well as the Jews.

4. *The Asian Pentecost*—Acts 19:1-7

The 12 disciples here were followers of John the Baptizer and have never heard of the Holy Spirit.

Paul detected something was wrong.

We are observing a confirmatory drama on a unique occasion.

The following points suggest the uniqueness of this event:
•These twelve men were not Christians in the proper sense.
•Their understanding of the gospel was incomplete.
•Paul's hands identified him with these converts and the Holy Spirit confirmed their acceptance.
•This was the first time the gospel had been preached in this new area of the world.
•Due to the occult atmosphere of Ephesus it was important that some singular sign of authenticity be given.

(It should be noted that there is no typical order of events in Acts which can be regarded as a pattern sequence. In any case, remember, Acts is a narrative portion of Scripture.)

5. *Praying for the Holy Spirit*—Luke 11:13

Note the discussion of the actual text (pages 197-198).

In any case this was prior to the outpouring of the Holy Spirit on all believers at Pentecost. The experience of believers before the birthday of the Church must not be made typical for today.

6. *One Baptism*—Ephesians 4:3-5
Question
Is Paul talking about "baptism in the Spirit" or "baptism in water" here?
Answer
Probably neither, in that particular sense. The apostle in this context is simply saying that there is only one baptism—call it "Christian baptism" if you will. There is not one baptism for Jews and another for Gentiles. The same Holy Spirit has incorporated both in the Body and it is this that both confess in their public water baptism.

Conclusion
These passages must be carefully understood in their historical context.
They do not support the view that Spirit baptism is subsequent to conversion.
They simply tell us what happened in certain unique historical situations.

Study 22

PUPPETS OR
PEOPLE?

/

Scripture: Hebrews 12:1-11
Memory: Philippians 3:13-14
Textbook: pages 199-204

Introduction
In this short study we consider some of the practical problems arising from the dangerous teaching that a person may be a Christian yet not have received the Holy Spirit. These problems include:

1. *Unhealthy, Morbid Introspection*
A Christian who is told that it is obvious he has not received the baptism of the Holy Spirit because he does not speak in tongues, etc., may well be upset. He may begin delving within himself to discover why he has missed this "essential experience." Such introspection is morbid and can have serious psychological and physical, not to mention spiritual, repercussions.
•*Antidote*
Refuse all opinions which are based on personal experience rather than on Scripture.
Remember God is more concerned that we read and believe His Word than that we "experience excitement."
Do not believe the high-sounding nonsensical claims of some high-powered TV "Christian" entrepreneurs.

2. *Frustration*

There is the very real danger we may begin to think God has cheated us. This leads to frustration and unholy discontent.

•*Antidote*

Quit asking God for blessings we already possess. Thank Him for them.

Understand that if God has "blessed us with *all* spiritual blessings ... in Christ"—and He *has* (Ephesians 1:3)—He has certainly not cheated us.

Pray for a contented spirit and a diligent mind to search the Scriptures.

3. *Wrong Sense of Values*

This erroneous teaching places more value on miraculous phenomena than on moral virtue.

•*Antidote*

Cultivate the fruit of the Spirit and shun fleshly ostentation.

Remember that: "the incorruptible apparel of a meek and quiet spirit . . . is in the sight of God of great price" (1 Peter 3:4 RV).

4. *Confusion*

People who hold this opinion usually mistake spiritual gifts for spirituality. Their priority becomes "happenings" rather than holiness.

•*Antidote*

Understand that carnal Christians may still have many gifts (cf., 1 Corinthians 1:4-7 and 3:3).

Realize that Scripture never exhorts us as individual Christians to pray for the Holy Spirit, for spiritual gifts, or for visible signs of divine approval.

Discover and use your God-given gift in the sphere of His choice.

5. *Wrong Emphasis*

There is an unscriptural emphasis on the Holy Spirit rather than a heart occupation with Christ.

•*Antidote*

Examine Scripture and discover that, while the Holy Spirit is essentially God and in no sense inferior to the Son, His ministry is to glorify Christ (John 15:26; 16:14-15; 16:13).

Enthrone Jesus Christ as Lord. Do not become obsessed with "experiences of the Spirit" (1 Corinthians 12:3).

6. *Conceit*

People who claim to have "arrived" spiritually tend to regard themselves as a kind of Christian elite. Their personal conceit may even lead them to "look down on" or "feel sorry for" others.

•*Antidote*

Cast pride away and remember that one of the fruits of the Spirit is "meekness" (the opposite of conceit!)

7. *Apathy*

People who have attained the ultimate in spiritual "highs" easily become apathetic. If I consider myself to have "arrived," what else is there? Hence comes the "let-down."

•*Antidote*

Realize that while we may enjoy a victorious Christian life we shall never reach perfection here.

Understand that God's will is for us to be "pressing toward the mark" (Philippians 3:14); "looking [off] unto Jesus" (Hebrews 12:2); and patiently running the race (Hebrews 12:1). There is no room for apathy here!

8. *Division*

This "second blessing" doctrine divides Christians and destroys fellowship within and between churches.

•*Antidote*

Seek to maintain "the unity of the Spirit in the bond of peace" (Ephesians 4:3).

Be sure to find a church home where Christ is recognized as Head and where everything is tested by the touchstone of Scripture.

Summary

Any spiritual experience which tends to have a deleterious effect upon our mind, emotions, or physical health must be suspect.

Study 23

GOD'S MIGHTY WORKS

Scripture: Acts 2:1-21
Memory: Acts 2:42
Textbook: pages 205-221

Introduction

Any discussion of the highly controversial subject of glossolalia is likely to engender "heat." It is important to understand the position taken in this Study Guide.

In the text, *The Holy Spirit: Lord and Life-Giver*, the subject of "Speaking in Tongues" is dealt with fairly extensively and with constant reference to Scripture. The author does not accept that tongues are part of God's plan for the Church today. He seeks to avoid dogmatism but is quite firm in his point of view. This may be summarized as follows:

1. The contemporary emphasis on tongues is a sellout to subjectivism.

2. Tongues, far from being a criterion of spirituality, may well be a sign of carnality or even divine judgment.

3. A careful examination of Scripture will reveal that the current teaching about tongues being a sign of Spirit baptism, and that they are to be sought after by Christians today, is wrong doctrine. It should be labeled "erroneous," not "optional," by evangelical Christians.

4. While the topic should be discussed in Christian love, love is not blind to truth. Christians need to be much more mature and decisive in dealing with this issue.

1. *The Biblical Data*
   Acts 2—The Day of Pentecost
   1 Corinthians 12—14—Paul's regulations of the Corinthian glossolalia.
   Acts 10:46—The House of Cornelius
   Acts 19:6—The Ephesian Twelve
   These are discussed in chapter 22 of the textbook, pages 189-198.

   Note Mark 16:17—the textual integrity of this passage is suspect and is better omitted from this discussion. For a careful treatment of this matter read Biblical commentaries. For example, Cole writes: "It would be unwise to build any theological position upon these verses alone; and this no responsible Christian group has done" (*Tyndale New Testament Commentary*: Mark. R.A. Cole, pages 257-259; cf., *New International Commentary*: Mark. W.L. Lane, pages 601-605).

   For another point of view see *An Analysis of the Gospel of Mark*, Harold St. John, pages 172-173.

2. *Terms*—(may be usefully reviewed)
   • "Glossolalia" means "speaking in tongues" and is derived from *glōssa* (tongue) and *laleō* (to speak).
   • "Subjectivism" teaches that knowledge is derived from personal experience and cannot be tested by external or objective criteria.
   • "Polyglot" means multilingual or speaking many languages.
   • "Xenolalia" means speaking in foreign languages (from Greek *xenos*, stranger).
   • "Didactic" Scriptures—teaching or instructional passages. These are in contrast with the narrative or story-telling passages.
   • "Hermeneutics" is the science of Biblical interpretation.
   • "Linguistics" means the study of languages.
   • "Normative" means that which sets the standard.

3. *Glossolalia on the Day of Pentecost*—(read Acts 2:4-11)
   • A singular supernatural act of the Holy Spirit.
   • Intelligibility dependent on more than linguistics.
   • Predisposed the congregation to hear the gospel.
   • It was a miracle of speech rather than hearing.
   • Luke's term *dialēktos* (verses 6,8, etc. cf., dialect) is unequivocal. It

means language or dialect.

•In Jewish rabbinic tradition the Feast of Pentecost commemorated the giving of the Law at Sinai.

4. *The Disorder at Corinth*—1 Corinthians 12—14

Paul attempts to regulate an abuse of tongues at Corinth by warning of its dangers and pointing out its relative unimportance.

Significantly, there is no reference to tongues in any other of Paul's correspondence. This is significant particularly in the light of Romans 12 and Ephesians 4 (other gift lists).

•*Apostolic Guidelines* (1 Corinthians 12—14). Given in answer to specific questions.

The Holy Spirit is sovereign in His disposition of gifts—1 Corinthians 12:4-11.

Not all Christians (even then) should expect tongues—1 Corinthians 12:10,30.

Tongues comparatively insignificant—last on list!—1 Corinthians 14:5.

Intelligibility is crucial in communication—1 Corinthians 14:19.

Abandonment of personal control is dangerous—1 Corinthians 14:30-32.

Tongues were a sign for the immature—1 Corinthians 14:22.

Tongues intelligible without interpreter.

Praying or singing must be with the intellect—1 Corinthians 14:20.

Corporate edification is the criterion.

Tongues must be controlled (at Corinth!)—1 Corinthians 14:5,28.

•*Apostolic Regulations* (1 Corinthians 14)

No tongues without an interpreter. (It was the content that mattered, not the process. Tongues proved nothing.)

Must be restricted to two or three speakers (maximum).

Must be sequential.

No indiscriminate, involuntary use of tongues.

Avoid confusion at all cost.

•*Comparison of the Pentecost and Corinthian Glossolalia.*

Question

Were these different phenomena?

Answer

Yes!

F.F. Bruce (Reylands Professor of Biblical Criticism and Exegesis, University of Manchester) suggests that at Pentecost the result of glossolalia was better understanding, but evidently not so at Corinth.

Leon Morris (Principal, Ridley College, Melbourne) suggests that at Pentecost the apostles spoke known languages whereas at Corinth it appears to be ecstatic speech.

Ralph Martin, (New Testament Professor, Fuller Seminary, California) suggests these are two different phenomena.

Answer

No!

R.G. Gromacki (author, *The Modern Tongues Movement*) believes that although "ecstatic tongues" is one possible meaning of *glōssa* this is still inconclusive (see quote textbook page 216). He argues that since Luke and Paul both use the same Greek word they are talking about the same thing. He also sees *gēne glōssōn* (1 Corinthians 12:10) as conclusive (cf., quote page 216).

It would seem that the weight of informed opinion is on behalf of these phenomena being different.

5. *A Comparison Between Modern Teaching and the New Testament*

Modern View	*New Testament Teaching*
•Tongues is an evidence of the baptism of the Holy Spirit.	•All Christians have been baptized in the Holy Spirit.
	Not all Christians speak in tongues.
	For a conclusive answer read 1 Corinthians 12:13. Here Paul states, "we were *all* baptized," yet in verse 30 he clearly implies not *all* speak in tongues (read textbook page 217).
•Tongues: a sign of spirituality.	•The people who were speaking in tongues at Corinth were carnal! (cf., 1 Corinthians 3:1,3)
•Exalts tongues as the ultimate.	•Paul plays it down (1 Corinthians 14:5,9,14,19,23).
•Quite unrestrained and public (in this writer's experience).	•Strictly controlled and rather private.
•The "quiescent mind" approach to tongues is encouraged.	•The idea of having the mind in "animated suspension" would be anathema to Paul (1 Corinthians 14:20,14,15,32).
•"The more the merrier" appears to be the approach. If there is confusion, so be it!	•The Scripture stringently regulates (cf., 1 Corinthians 14).
•"Wait, tarry, strive, struggle to get this experience" is the usual attitude.	•The New Testament sees tongues as a gift in the early church—not a reward for trying!
•Paul wanted everyone to speak in tongues like himself.	•Paul clearly says he would prefer people to prophesy! (See explanation pages 220-221.)

GROWING ON
TO MATURITY

Scripture: 1 Corinthians 13
Memory: 1 Corinthians 14:20
Textbook: pages 221-235

Introduction

In our last study we looked at the New Testament data regarding tongues and attempted to discover Paul's principles in regard to this topic. We also looked at the strange teachings and frenetic activities of modern charismatics in the light of the Scriptures.

Here we must try to establish some perspectives and make an evaluation.

1. *Perspectives*

•The experiences of people, whether they be famous contemporaries or historical Biblical characters, must not be considered normative. Scripture is our only authoritative and absolute criterion.

•It is important to distinguish between narrative portions of Scripture (e.g., Gospels, Acts, etc.) and those that are didactic (e.g., Epistles).

•To say that God may not act today as He did in the primitive (precanonical) church suggests God's sovereign choice and variety of dealing. It does not limit God.

•Scripture is final and self-authenticating. It does not require corroborating signs. Signs would help authenticate precanonical revelation. The primitive church did not have a complete Bible.

•Hermeneutics requires that Scripture be interpreted contextually.

•The ministry of the Holy Spirit is to glorify and exalt Christ. Any teaching therefore which lays undue stress on the Holy Spirit at the expense of presenting Christ is to be regarded with suspicion.

•The tongues emphasis at Corinth will be best understood if we see them against the backdrop of the pagan frenzies and religious orgies of that city.

•The sign gifts were clearly suited to the Jewish atmosphere of the New Testament churches. Once the transition era (approximately until A.D. 50) of the church was past, and Gentiles fully recognized as fellow members, the evidence is the sign gifts ceased.

•Evidently not all New Testament Christians used tongues. Therefore if the gift was not universal in days prior to the completion of the canon of Scripture, why insist on its being so today?

•While Paul had enjoyed a facility in tongues, this evidently ceased.

2. *Evaluation*

"Tongues not for today"

•Paul predicted the cessation of tongues. Note his different verbs in 1 Corinthians 13:8:

Prophecy and knowledge—shall be done away (*katargēthēsontai*, literally, shall be superseded).

Tongues—"will cease" (*pausontai*, literally, will stop) (see discussion in textbook, pages 225-226).

Church history confirms that tongues ceased (see Smeaton quote page 227).

•The apostle associates the cessation of the partial revelation of knowledge, prophecy, and tongues with the arrival of the completed canon. (That this is his sense is discussed fully—read pages 227-230).

The popular attempt to explain this away by making "that which is complete" (*to teleion*) refer to the hereafter is untenable as far as the Greek of Paul's passage is concerned. Nor does it make sense in the light of Paul's words about faith, hope, and love abiding. We shall not need faith and hope in Heaven!

•Even in his day Paul advocated that the Church earnestly desire that the greater (not the lesser!) gifts be manifest among them—and always in the atmosphere of love (1 Corinthians 12:31 RV). Why seek anything different today?

•Tongues may simply be a "crutch" for people who refuse to believe and accept God's Word for its own sake.

This is the point of the quotation from Isaiah 28 (see discussion, pages 231-233).

•If tongues had been of lasting value and for today then the obvious place for their use as media of communication would be the foreign mission field. The clear evidence is that missionaries communicate in languages they learn through arduous academic toil, not through "tongues."

•The New Testament is clear that the sign gifts were apostolic and belonging to the foundational era of the Church (2 Corinthians 12:12; Hebrews 2:3-4, etc.)

•It is strange reasoning which suggests that the divinely-given gift of speech should give way to a cacaphony of gibberish in order to demonstrate the presence of the Holy Spirit.

•Since all kinds of pagan religious and Christless cults practice glossolalia, this phenomenon of itself proves absolutely nothing.

•The practice of glossolalia with its emphasis on subjectivism is almost always divisive. Such teaching is best avoided (Romans 16:17, see Amplified Version).

•The Christian's basic need is to grow in grace and in the knowledge of Christ, always abounding in love.

WHEN HE
IS COME

/

Scripture: Psalm 104
Memory: John 16:8-11
Textbook: pages 237-246

In this study we consider the three areas of the Spirit's work in relation to the world:
Creation
Conviction
Conversion

In this context "world" means:
Earth as part of material creation
Mankind

1. *Creation*
The Trinity is involved in creation:
•The Father is viewed as Author and Source (Romans 11:36)
•The Son as the Divine Agent in Creation (John 1:3; Colossians 1:16-17)
•The Holy Spirit as the Instrument and Life-Giver (Psalm 104:29-30)
The Holy Spirit's creative work is noted in:
•Genesis 1:2 (see Job 26:13)
The Spirit "brooding," "fluttering." Here is the picture of a mother bird caring for her brood.
•Psalm 104:29-30; Job 34:14; Ecclesiastes 12:7
In these verses the idea is of the creative life-breath of the Spirit.
•Job 33:4; Genesis 2:7; Job 32:8
Here the Spirit is seen as the Creator of man's life, including his mind and spirit.

2. *Conviction*
Another work of the Holy Spirit in relation to the world of men is that of conviction. He uses the media of:
Conscience
Scripture
Experience
This is probably the thought behind the phrase about Scripture being "the sword of the Spirit." God's Word exposes, probes, discerns, divides, and makes man aware of his sin.
Read:
Hebrews 4:12-13
Acts 2:37 (Peter)
Acts 7:54 (Stephen)

Our Lord reveals three aspects of the Spirit's conviction of the world:
•Sin—because of failure to believe on Christ.
•Righteousness—that is the failure of human goodness to satisfy God and the sufficiency of Christ's righteousness now made available because of His completed work.
•Judgment (N.B. not "judgment to come")—because although Satan is defeated, men still submit to him and refuse Christ.

3. *Conversion*
This does not mean that the world as a whole will be converted. Rather it stresses the truth that salvation is a work of the Holy Spirit from first to last.
•He points men to Christ (John 15:26)
Consider the means He uses—e.g., Spirit-filled men (verse 27)
•He demonstrates the truth of the gospel
Without the Spirit's work man is blind to spiritual truth (see John 3:3 and 1 Corinthians 2:11-14 RV)
Historically He did this by "signs following"—e.g., Acts 2:2-4; 8:14-17; 10:44; 14:3; etc.
Now He does it through the inspired Word (2 Timothy 3:16)
•He effects the new birth
The subject of regeneration is dealt with elsewhere (cf., Study 14) but it is referred to here to emphasize that it is the Spirit's work.
Conversion or rebirth results when the Spirit of God moves on man's will, reveals Christ, and plants the incorruptible seed of the Word of God (read John 3; 1 Peter 1:22-23).
In confirmation of this change described by Paul as "beginning in the Spirit" (Galatians 3:3), the Holy Spirit witnesses with the regenerate person's Spirit that he is in God's family (Romans 8:16).

Read Chapter 25 in the textbook.

A Warning
A man must beware of hardening his heart against the Spirit and thus forfeiting His gracious presence. See Genesis 6:3; Exodus 8:32; 9:12; 1 Timothy 4:2; and Romans 1:28.

Study 26

ISRAEL MY
SERVANT
/ Scripture: Isaiah 63:7-14
Memory: Zechariah 4:6
Textbook: pages 247-254

Introduction
We must beware of thinking that because the post-Pentecost era is described as "the Age of the Spirit," the Holy Spirit was not at work before that time. Scripture plainly teaches that throughout the history of God's chosen people Israel, the Spirit has been there. In this study we shall examine how His presence was made manifest.

1. *The Spirit Indwelling Israel*
   Haggai 2:4-5; Isaiah 63:6-14; Exodus 15:8-10; 2 Samuel 22:16
   •The Spirit was with Israel in Egypt
   •He was with them in the Exodus
   •He brought them through the sea
   •He settled them in Canaan

2. *The Spirit Endues Israel's Leaders*
   In Old Testament times the Spirit appears to have come upon men temporarily giving enabling for specific tasks.
   Bezaleel—to build the tabernacle—Exodus 31:3
   The priests (anointing)—for service—Exodus 29:20-21 cf., verse 7
   The judges—for delivering the nation—Judges 6:34; 14:6; 14:19; etc.
   The kings—to rule—e.g., 1 Samuel 16:13, etc.
   It would be useful to list the many references to this special enduement (in Old Testament).

3. *The Spirit Inspired Israel's Prophets*
   •For oral prophecy (cf., Nehemiah 9:30 RV, Acts 28:25-26)
   Azariah—2 Chronicles 15:1
   Micah—Micah 3:8
   Ezekiel—Ezekiel 11:5,24
   Balaam—Numbers 24:2,25
   •For written prophecy (cf., 1 Peter 1:21)
   The former prophets (cf., 1 Samuel 10:10—Zechariah 7:12; David—2 Samuel 23:2
   (New Testament corroboration—Matthew 22:43; Acts 1:16)

4. *The Spirit Delivered and Restored Israel* (read all references)
   Zechariah 4:6

61

Isaiah 59:19
Ezekiel 37:9-14
Joel 2:28-29
These verses had a partial fulfillment in the postexilic restoration but await complete fulfillment when Messiah returns.

5. *The Spirit Anoints Israel's Messiah*
Isaiah 11:1-2—Note the sevenfold anointing and compare Revelation 1:4; 3:1; and 5:6
Spirit of the Lord
  Wisdom
  Understanding
  Counsel
  Might
  Knowledge
  Fear of the Lord
As "The Servant of Jehovah"
Isaiah 61:1—(cf., Luke 4:18,21)
Isaiah 48:16—this verse suggests not only the Spirit's association with Messiah but also his separate identity.
Note the careful wording of the Aaronic benediction—Numbers 6:24-26—and compare the trinitarian benediction of 2 Corinthians 13:14 (cf., Matthew 28:19).

Study 27

DONT PLAY GAMES WITH GOD!

/

Scripture: Matthew 12:22-37
Memory: Ephesians 4:30
Textbook: pages 255-260

Since the Holy Spirit is God He can be sinned against. Scripture mentions at least five areas in which He may be sinned against:
1. Blasphemy against the Holy Spirit
2. Quenching the Holy Spirit
3. Grieving the Holy Spirit
4. Resisting the Holy Spirit
5. Lying to the Holy Spirit
Sins against the Holy Spirit appear to be in the nature of sins of commission rather than sins of omission.

1. *Blasphemy Against the Spirit*—Matthew 12:31

This is the most notorious of sins against the Spirit and is often described as "the unpardonable sin."

This serious charge arose when certain Pharisees, in an attempt to slight Jesus, attributed His Spirit-inspired works to Satan. (Examine the story carefully.)

A frequent question: Can we commit the unpardonable sin today? In answer note the following:

•The charge arose in a certain set of historical circumstances.

•Jesus' contemporaries had unique evidence offered them which left them without excuse.

•If, as is evident from Scripture, a Christian is indwelt and sealed by the Holy Spirit, it is obvious that he cannot commit an unpardonable sin.

•Anyone who worries whether he has committed such a sin clearly has not, otherwise the Spirit would not still be present to convict of sin.

Two things are important.

Jesus did not say anyone *had committed* the unpardonable sin. He warned against it and explained it. Therefore we shall be wise to refrain from dogmatizing.

The only way to put ourselves beyond the place of forgiveness today is to refuse Christ—see 1 John 5:10-12, also John 3:36.

2. *Quenching the Spirit*

The picture is one of putting out a fire. We may be guilty of "quenching the Spirit" when:

•We refuse God's Word.

•We frustrate God's work by obstinacy, or traditionalism.

•We criticize one of the Lord's servants.

•We disobey the Spirit's promptings.

3. *Grieving the Spirit*

Paul recognizes this possibility in Ephesians 4:30.

To describe this as "sinning against the Spirit" may be an overstatement.

Here we are not so much concerned with the deity and sovereignty of the Spirit as with that very personal relationship we have with Him.

You can only "grieve" a person who loves you very much.

4. *Lying to the Holy Spirit*

Again this sin is linked to a specific historical situation (Acts 5:3).

5. *Resisting the Holy Spirit*

This is viewed in Scripture as Israel's national sin—Isaiah 63:10; Acts 7:51.

Christians may also be rebellious.

FOR FURTHER STUDY

Please refer to Part VII. The Holy Spirit in the Scriptures (pages 261-279).

In this part of the book, *The Holy Spirit: Lord and Life-Giver*, the Bible student will find a comprehensive analysis of the Biblical references to the Person and work of the Holy Spirit.

There are eleven study outlines, each with a short introductory paragraph followed by analytical headings and references.

While not exhaustive, in the sense of a concordance, this section contains almost all references to the Holy Spirit in both the Old and New Testaments.

This section of the book can be used in various ways.

1. As the text for a group study or Biblical teaching about the Holy Spirit.

2. As a personal daily study guide over a three-to-six-month period.

3. As a topical reference guide to the subject of the Holy Spirit.

For list of study outlines see textbook page 263.

Notes

Notes

Notes

Notes

Notes

Notes

Notes

Notes